SPORT IN THE GLOBAL SOCIETY
General Editors: J.A. Mangan and Boria Majumdar

LOST HISTORIES OF INDIAN CRICKET

SPORT IN THE GLOBAL SOCIETY
General Editors: J.A. Mangan and Boria Majumdar

The interest in sports studies around the world is growing and will continue to do so. This unique series combines aspects of the expanding study of *sport in the global society*, providing comprehensiveness and comparison under one editorial umbrella. It is particularly timely, with studies in the cultural, economic, ethnographic, geographical, political, social, anthropological, sociological and aesthetic elements of sport proliferating in institutions of higher education.

Eric Hobsbawm once called sport one of the most significant practices of the late nineteenth century. Its significance was even more marked in the late twentieth century and will continue to grow in importance into the new millennium as the world develops into a 'global village' sharing the English language, technology and sport.

Other Titles in the Series

LOST HISTORIES OF INDIAN CRICKET

Battles off the Pitch

by

Boria Majumdar

Routledge
Taylor & Francis Group

LONDON AND NEW YORK

This edition first published 2006 by Routledge
2 Park Square, Milton Park,
Abingdon, Oxon, OX14 4RN

Simultaneously published in the USA and Canada
by Taylor & Francis Inc

270 Madison Ave,
New York, NY 10016

Routledge is an imprint of the Taylor & Francis Group

© 2006 Boria Majumdar

South Asian edition published by YODA PRESS, G 93, Connaught Circus,
New Delhi 110 001, India (www.yodapress.com), 2004.

Typeset in ClassGaramond BT by Excellent Laser Typesetters, Delhi
Printed and bound in Great Britain by TJ International Ltd, Padstow, Cornwall

This edition is not for sale in South Asia
(India, Pakistan, Bangladesh, Myanmar, Bhutan, Nepal and Sri Lanka).

Every effort has been made to ensure that the advice and information in this book is
true and accurate at the time of going to press. However, neither the publisher nor the
authors can accept any legal responsibility or liability for any errors or omissions that
may be made. In the case of drug administration, any medical procedure or the use of
technical equipment mentioned within this book, you are strongly advised to consult the
manufacturer's guidelines.

British Library Cataloguing in Publication Data
A catalogue record for this book is available from the British Library

Library of Congress Cataloging in Publication Data

A catalog record has been requested

ISBN 0-415-35885-X (hbk)
ISBN 0-415-35886-8 (pbk)

For Sharmistha – who is often forced
to live and breathe cricket with me.

Contents

Acknowledgements

Thanks are especially due to my friends at Wisden Asia. The Editor, Sambit Bal, was instrumental in helping me plan this book when I first met him in Bombay—my thanks to him. Many, knowingly or unknowingly, have helped me on the way. I have learnt a great deal from the collections of Raju Mukherjee, Anandji Dossa, Moti Nandi, Khalid Ansari, Theo Braganza, and Vasant Raiji. Access to the Board of Control for Cricket in India archives and papers, essential for this book, would have been impossible without the help and support of Mr. Jagmohan Dalmiya. Sincere thanks is due to my friend and senior colleague, J.A. Mangan, for having read numerous earlier drafts. Finally, this book would not have been completed without the help of my colleagues at Taylor and Francis, Samantha Grant, Jon Manley, Kate Manson and Lucille Murby. It has been wonderful to work with them.

Boria Majumdar
October 2005

Series Editor's Foreword

Let us be honest: South Asia (specifically India) is fast becoming the centre of world cricket with its wealthy, idolised players, its numerous enraptured followers and above all, its advancing commercial power and, while if in the past nugatory recognition was the lot of Indian cricket writers, this too is fast becoming a thing of the past. Permit me a prophecy: no one will consolidate this change of status faster than the talented, young Boria Majumdar already the author of the official history of Indian cricket, *Twenty Two Yards to Freedom*. For my part, when I made his acquaintance some little time ago, Keatsian-like:

> Then felt I like some watcher in the skies
> When a new planet swims into his ken.[1]

Lost Histories of Indian Cricket reveals a knowledge that is impressively encyclopaedic and a passion that is seductively intense. Now a challenge faces the author that I know he will relish: to blend with grace, generosity and completeness the significant imperial and post-imperial cricketing moments of the whole subcontinent into a seamless story and bring back to life those across the entire subcontinent of all colours, creeds and nationalities, who gave determined birth to the game there, nurtured it with sustained affection and so helped bring it to its present popularity. Covert continuities need to be made overt—and he is the one to do it.

Lost Histories has many virtues but candour has primacy. *Lost Histories* is delightfully honest. Warts appear beside beauty spots. 'How many natures lie in human nature', Pascal once famously remarked. Many of their by-products are to be found in *Lost Histories*: imperialism, nationalism, regionalism, factionalism, violent and non-violent protest, self-serving and self-interest, animosities and rivalries, but also co-operation, conciliation, altruism, amity and allegiance. And if there is one thing *Lost Histories* makes crystal-clear it is that in India cricket is often politics and politics is often cricket. This sempiternal reality is recorded with a frankness that wins applause. There is no whitewashed wall!

In sum, *Lost Histories* is a work of sharp-eyed prescience. By way of illustration, let's leave almost the last word to its impressive author: 'In modern India, no hyperbole is sufficient to capture the importance of cricket in the country's national life.... Cricket is the only realm where Indians can flex their muscles on the world stage: it is the nation's only instrument with which to have a crack at world domination. It is, to put it simply, much more than a 'game' for Indians. Such an intense engagement with this wonderful game began more than a century ago, and if anything, it promises to become even more energetic over the coming decades...'[2]

In the years ahead, one thing is certain: the author of *Lost Histories* will bring his own intense engagement to this 'intense engagement' and record this *scène à faire* with magisterial authority.

Swanage, 2005   J.A. MANGAN
                                                                 Series Editor

Prologue

'Cricket is an Indian game accidentally discovered by the English.' So says Ashis Nandy, before going on to add that to most Indians the game now looks more Indian than English. In fact cricket today arouses more passions in India than in England or any other cricket-playing country in the world.

Yet, when it comes to writing on the game, we Indians still continue to take a backseat. This leads us to look upon British and Australian writers as masters of cricket literature, in complete ignorance of our own written traditions. British and Australian cricket histories are still much revered, and books on Indian cricket, few and far between, merit their place in shops that market the penny press. While writers like Robertson Glasgow, E.V. Lucas, John Arlott and the legendary Neville Cardus duly deserve their places in cricket's hall of fame, some Indians like J.C. Maitra, Berry Sarbadhikary and J.M. Ganguly, many of whom were day-to-day historians of the game, are also worthy of appreciation. These Indians, who had written on the game for years in newspapers and journals, have been accorded limited recognition, which is nugatory in comparison to their British and Australian counterparts. This oversight has not only led us to ignore our own writers and critics, it has also led to the obscuring of many fascinating cricketing chapters of the past. Stories and tales, which deserve mention in the annals of our cricket history, have been relegated to the dusty shelves of archives. Many of these 'past furores' are captivating stories of intrigue and power play, machinations that would enrich writers of paperback thrillers to say the least. Yet, these controversies of yesteryears have faded away into oblivion. While cricket enthusiasts are familiar with names like Ranji, Duleep and the Nawab of Pataudi, umpires like P.B. Jog and M.G. Bhave, administrators like A.S. De Mello and writers like Shapoorjee Sorabjee continue to be unheard of. These men, the following pages will demonstrate, were no less colourful and played no less important parts in the unfolding of that saga we now designate 'The History of Indian Cricket'. Without referring to the tract written by Shapoorjee Sorabjee in 1897, any history of cricket in India remains incomplete. That a slight injury to an European lady was enough for the police commissioner to stop natives from playing cricket in Bombay, and that bands were kept in attendance during prize cricket matches of the 1870s, are pieces of information that Shapoorjee Sorabjee has left us with. While people know of the *Jubilee Book* written by Ranji in 1897, they hardly know why Ranji wrote the book in the first place. The book, an integral part of his broader scheme to win back the Jamnagar *Gadi*, portrays Ranji as no less able a strategist than Chanakya.

It is common knowledge that the first Indians to play cricket in India were the Parsees of Bombay. To further their cricketing prowess, the Parsees decided to undertake a tour of Britain in 1878, an initiative that failed to take off. While existing monographs refer to this failed initiative, the reason behind this failure remains unknown to most observers and commentators. It is interesting to note that the project fell through under extremely unfortunate circumstances, on account of a dispute between A.B. Patel, the man who was the main mover behind the tour, and K.N. Kabraji, leading ultimately to a libel suit. In a similar vein, we often wonder why the two Parsee teams that toured England in 1886 and 1888 fared so differently from each other. On the first tour, the Indians won a solitary match, while in the second, they showed a marked improvement winning eight of their encounters. The reason is that the team that visited England in 1886 was by no means representative of the best Parsee talent available in the country. The team was not selected, and was made up of cricket enthusiasts who were willing to pay for their expenses on the tour.

All British counties have histories of their own; the county championship has numerous histories that speak of its heritage and contribution to developing the game in England. In contrast, the Bombay Pentangular, the foremost tournament in pre-Partition India, continues to languish with a solitary history. The story of its abolition, no less sensational than a Hollywood mystery, has largely passed unnoticed. It is interesting to note that the first Presidency match played in 1892 (the earliest variant of the Pentangular) was known as the 'Fire Engine' match. The reason was that fire engines had to be solicited to drain rainwater from the ground to facilitate the start of the match.

While Bodyline remains the most celebrated cricket controversy ever, rivalled in recent times by match fixing, the numer-ous controversies that Lala Amarnath was involved in go unmentioned in books of cricket history, hardly ever discussed by researchers and enthusiasts. The charge levelled by the Board President, A.S. De Mello, that Amarnath accepted a purse of Rs. 5,000 from cricket enthusiasts in Calcutta to include Probir Sen of Bengal in the Indian test team against the West Indies and the 27,000-word rejoinder by Amarnath, published in 19 separate instalments by a leading national daily, has no parallel in other cricket-playing countries of the world. In no cricket-playing nation was the country's leading cricketer dropped on the morning of a Test match without being informed, and the umpire forced to give up half his remuneration if he wished to stand in future games. Also, nowhere else was a captain suspended for selling a match in the 1940s. Indian cricket history is replete with such instances; incidents that make one sit up and ask, 'Was this really possible?' Yet, for some inexplicable reason these incidents have escaped the attention of observers, enthusiasts and scholars.

Most chapters in this book are based on newspaper accounts, reported in the leading dailies by journalists, whom I call the day-to-day historians of the game. While such newspaper reportage has its limitations, influenced as it is by personal preferences and contemporary perspective, it remains of considerable value for any work on the history of Indian cricket.

Recently, a British friend of mine, more passionate about Rabindranath Tagore than most of us Indians here at Oxford, asked me, 'Is there any sphere in India where this legend has not left his mark?' 'I am sure Tagore had nothing to do with cricket,' another one piped up, noticing me (a cricket historian and Bengali to boot) at the same table. Cricket, he assumed, may well be that 'outcaste', one left untouched by Tagore. The incident reminded me of a story I had read many years ago, a story in an unpublished essay on the genesis of sports journalism, which I would like to narrate here.

Brajaranjan Ray, the pioneer of sports journalism in Bengali, recounts his experience in this unpublished essay I had the fortune of reading. Apparently, he found himself at a loss trying to look for Bengali equivalents of English terms in describing/reporting cricket matches. And who else to turn to but Tagore?

Tagore was encouraging as ever and asked him to go ahead without fear, inventing terminology. With his customary astuteness he assumed correctly that whatever Ray coined and persisted with, would, with the passage of time, become standard usage. Ray of course was free to turn to him for advice and corrections.

And that is not all. Apart from this Ray–Tagore encounter of the 1930s, there is also an imaginary match apparently played some time in the 1930s (fascinatingly described in a piece—loosely translated as *Rabindranath and Cricket*—sometime in the 1950s in *Dainik Basumati*, a Bengali journal, and later reprinted in some collections) that I was and am reminded of.

The setting of the match is Gomoh, a small town near Dhanbad, Bihar, more famous for its railway station from which Subhash Chandra Bose took his train towards Europe. What the writer of the piece would have us believe is that Tagore had gone there for a brief visit and had decided to organise a cricket match. The players who played against Tagore's team included such luminaries as Vizzy, the Maharajkumar of Vizianagram; the Maharaja of Patiala; Pataudi Senior; the Maharaja of Cooch Behar and Duleepsinhji. They apparently all arrived in their private jets, a point much emphasised in the piece.

That the celebrity players spent money to play the game, rather than playing to earn, does not need to be emphasised, but another interesting sidelight of the match was the bit about advertisements and promotions. In the 1930s, advertising was still in its infancy, but not, it seems, for this match. The author reports that the leading sports goods dealers from Bengal—S. Ray and Co., Uberoi et al.—had assembled in Gomoh with an extensive range of products.

The inaugural ceremony of the match began with a *shenai* recital, though the Maharaja of Patiala had also, it seems, arranged for a band to perform on the occasion. Two players from Tagore's side, Professor Kshiti Mohan Sen (father of our Nobel Laureate Amartya Sen) and Acharya Bidhusekhar Shastri recited vedic mantras to start off the proceedings. The stadium, a temporary arrangement for the match (typical of modern one-day internationals) was packed to capacity. Another key aspect of the match, one typical of modern cricket, was the presence of women spectators. They were all dressed in saris worn the Maharashtrian way. It is worth mentioning in this context that women in the 1930s played cricket in saris, and there was a regular tradition of cricket between men and women in Kathiawar. Also present for this match, were the great dancer Mani Behn, the famous motor racing specialist Rajkumari Sharmila, the daughters of the Gaekwad family, the Rajkumari of Burdwan and sundry other who's who.

Needless to mention, the event had to have nationalist overtones. So Rabindranath, inspired by swadeshi, played with a bat made from local wood, wore a *toka* (a headdress worn by peasants) made of palm-leaves and was dressed in a *dhoti*. Interestingly, this little detail cannot simply be dismissed as the anonymous writer's imagination, for cricket in *dhoti*s was very much in vogue in the 1930s and may well be perceived as an attempt by the Indians to appropriate cricket for nationalist purposes. (The Mohun Bagan Club did this in 1930 in a match against the Governors XI, and upon being reprimanded by R.B. Lagden for their dress refused to play. The match was eventually abandoned when Lagden refused to tender the apology demanded by Mohun Bagan. Six months later, a similar thing happened in a match between the Vidyasagar College and the Calcutta Cricket Club. On this occasion the Calcutta Club was forced to play with no other solution in sight.)

Instances such as the one referred to above have served as inspiration for the writing of this book. This volume, as I see it, seeks to enlighten Indian cricket fans about their lost cricketing past, drawing before them in broad brushstrokes lost pages of their cricket history, resuscitating forgotten heroes, both players and administrators.

Given modern cricket's political, economic and social potential, and its universal appeal across India, it is hardly surprising that the game plays a key role in contemporary society. As a result, governments, cricket's governing bodies and players, sponsors and fans, all try tenaciously to exert control over the game. Such tenaciousness is certain to result in future furores. In fact, a complete tale of controversies that have afflicted the game in India cannot be reproduced in a single volume, and the purpose of this book is to capture some of the more fascinating ones. As stories of all the controversies cannot be recounted here, it is intended that further instalments will appear in due course. Even then one might not be able to claim a complete and comprehensive documentation given the dynamic nature of Indian cricket. I sincerely hope that, in time, others will repair omissions to augment my efforts.

1
Empire vs. Parsee XI

Cricket in India has largely been looked upon as an alien sport appropriated as part of an emulative enterprise. The close link, if any, between cricket and nationalism is regarded as a contemporary phenomenon. Their linking, historically, is still looked upon as an unfounded proposition, evident from the following comment by Richard Cashman:

> Indian nationalism was less radical, in a cultural sense, than Irish where the nationalists attacked cricket and other English sports as objectionable elements of colonial culture and patronised Gaelic sports instead. The Indian nationalist leaders attacked the political and economic aspects of British imperialism but retained an affection for some aspects of English culture.[1]

This view appears relevant for Bombay where the Parsees, the first Indian community to play cricket, used cricket as a ladder for social mobility within the colonial framework. However, as both Mihir Bose and Ramachandra Guha have shown, the cricket field in Bombay did become a site for indigenous assertion against the colonisers in the late 1870s and early 1880s.[2] To quote Guha:

> The agents of disruption were the European polo players.... The coming of the polo players [to that area of the maidan where the natives played cricket] led to a bitter protest by the native cricketers. Their struggle to evict polo from the maidan provides a fascinating window on the cultural life of Empire, and demonstrates how quickly and how energetically Indians had made cricket their game.[3]

This contest is described in detail in Shapoorjee Sorabjee's *A Chronicle of Cricket among Parsees and The Struggle: Polo versus Cricket* published in 1897. The struggle began in 1879 when a native cricketer first described, 'how the polo players enclosed their playing area with black flags, prohibiting native cricketers from playing within its boundaries'.[4] He suggested that, 'nearly two thirds of the parade ground is occupied by Europeans to the great inconvenience of the school boys wishing to play cricket.'[5]

Two years after this report, as Guha states, 'Shapoorjee Sorabjee wrote a letter of protest to the Bombay gymkhana on behalf of the Persian Cricket Club'. However, the Polo Secretary of the Gymkhana dismissed his complaint, asserting their determination to play polo as before. The contest continued till the mid-1880s and though the natives won a temporary victory in 1882 (an order was passed in April 1882 allowing the Parsees exclusive use of the Esplanade Parade ground),[6] this decree was revoked in 1883 permitting the European polo players to use the native cricket ground.[7] In this fight, which ended in a defeat for the natives, the Asian game of polo, Guha argues, 'became the emblem of patrician power, and the English sport indulged by the natives the mark of plebeian resistance'.[8]

Interestingly, as this chapter will demonstrate, the struggle between polo and cricket is not the only occasion when the cricket-playing natives of Bombay clashed with their European masters. The first such clash occurred in 1868 and arose out of the following incident:

> A random cricket ball struck, not in the least injuriously, the wife of a European police constable whilst enjoying a stroll round about the cricket field. The behest consequently was given by the Commissioner of Police that no more cricket should be allowed at the Oval, and the Parsee cricketers were thereupon driven away thence by the police. The helpless boys not knowing what to do next were quite nonplussed.[9]

Soon after this incident, as Shapoorjee Sorabjee states, 'Sir Joseph Arnould's arrival on the scene, as he came for his evening stroll, inspired hopes in them (the Parsee cricketers) and they related their grievance to him.'[10] Upon hearing the story, Arnould, who was Chief Justice of the Bombay High Court, addressed the following letter to the Editor of the *Bombay Gazette*:

> Sir, As I was taking my stroll this evening by the side of the Rotten Row, several Parsee lads came running up to inform me that their cricket in Mr. Belasis' Oval had been suddenly stopped by one having authority, in consequence of a stray ball having found its way as far as the carriage drive— I hope this is not so, or that if such order has been issued by 'an authority', some higher authority with more good sense will lose no time in rescinding it. We, English, no doubt are reputed to prefer taking our pleasure sadly and exclusively, but it must be a very un-English sport of exclusiveness that feels

itself annoyed by a few noisy games of cricket played in its neighborhood by Parsee school boys. Tastes differ: but for my part it does my heart good to see and hear these vigorous lads so earnest about their manly game. It shows that though the sons of exiles and traders, they still have running in their veins some of the old blood of Kaikhoshru, and Ardaseer, and Shapoor, whom we, after Greeks, prefer calling Cyrus, and Artaxerxes and Sapor. There Mr. Editor, topics are few, the weather is hot; I have dropped a ball before your bat; it is for you to knock it about with as much vigour as (not being a Parsee lad) can in this heat be expected of you.[11]

Arnould continued to support the natives in this agitation, evident from the following report in the *Bombay Gazette* of 28 May 1868:

It is a pity that the commissioner of police had thought it necessary to put a stop to the amusements of the young Parsee cricketers who have been in the habit of pitching their wickets, very much to their own benefit and amusement, and rarely, if at all, to the inconvenience of any one else, in the spacious oval on the Esplanade formed by the new Rotten Row. We are not aware of the purposes for which it was intended by Mr. Bellasis and his coadjutors that that large area of enclosed ground should be used, but if it is not to be available for such games as cricket (which the place just seems made for) we cannot imagine what else could be the object, for certainly those who walk there of an evening could be counted on one's fingers. The promenade at the beach, and the road at the other side of the Row take away all the pedestrians; and if the lusty youngsters who wield the bat and ball are banished from the Oval, the ground had better be sold at once as the sites for building purposes. We imagine that any inconvenience caused by the cricketers can only have been of the very slightest character, and certainly nothing more than cricket causes anywhere. It would be as unreasonable to put a stop to thoroughfare in the streets for fear of accidents as to enforce the prohibition we allude to.[12]

Pressured by such complaints from respectable Englishmen, the Police Commissioner, F.S. Soulter sent a rejoinder to the Editor of the *Gazette*:

Several letters having lately appeared in your paper, and in other journals, on the subject of the restriction, which I deemed it my duty to place upon the cricketing on the space within Rotten Row, I think it right to explain why the prohibition became necessary. The danger and constant annoyance caused to the public by the cricket playing within Rotten Row has frequently been represented to me, and I have on several occasions been an eyewitness to the fact myself. The Oval piece of ground within Rotten Row does not afford sufficient piece of ground for cricketing in safety, and the balls are therefore constantly hit beyond the rails on to the Rotten Row, and the young men fielding run in blind excitement right on to the riding ground, and probably just as people are galloping fast, and to the great danger of both the cricketer and the rider. There have been many narrow escapes in this manner, and although no serious accident has taken place up to the present time, sooner or later there will certainly be a mishap unless some restriction is put upon the cricketing. But apart from the necessity for prohibiting the cricketing as a mere measure of precaution to guard against accident to the public, the space for recreation has been so much curtailed by the loss of the sands, and other ground on the Esplanade taken up for building purposes, that it would be a gross injustice to the whole community if perhaps the very best piece of ground for recreation in Bombay should be wholly monopolized by a few cricketers to the entire exclusion of the public, particularly European and native ladies and children, who are at present debarred the use of this ground by fear of the cricket balls which fly about. I should be very sorry indeed to see the cricketers entirely deprived of the enjoyment of this manly game, but I think a piece of ground could be allotted to them on the Esplanade to the north side of the fort, and I have personally explained to the secretaries of the cricket clubs that there is no objection whatever to their using the ground within Rotten Row up to half past four or five 'o' clock in the afternoon.[13]

Eventually, as Shapoorjee Sorabjee declares, 'Notwithstanding the kind advocacy of Sir Joseph and the sympathetic support of the Bombay Gazette in favour of the occupation of the Oval by the Parsee cricketers, the best cricket ground in point of healthfulness in Bombay was thus mercilessly wrenched away from them.'[14]

As in the struggle between native cricket and European polo, in the clash between European recreation and native cricket, the colonised were forced to concede to the ruling English. However, in the third and final episode of the struggle in 1929–30, when native cricket administrators made common cause with the Gandhian call for civil disobedience, the English found themselves on the receiving end.

The final chapter of the struggle started when the Marylebone Cricket Club (MCC) was invited to tour India in November–December 1931.[15] This tour received full support from the Viceroy, Lord Irwin, evident from his letter to R.E. Grant-Govan, President of the Board of Control for Cricket in India (BCCI):

I am glad to learn that it is hoped to welcome a touring team this coming cold weather and that active arrangements are in progress for sending a team from India to England next summer. I trust that nothing will happen to prevent either of these enterprises and I shall watch their progress with much interest.[16]

The tour also received support from most cricket associations of the country. During its general body meeting, the Sind Cricket Association passed the following resolution in support of the tour: 'The committee has agreed to guarantee a sum of Rs 5000 to the Board of control for cricket in India in connection with the visit of the MCC to Karachi plus the percentage of profits equal to fifty percent of the guarantee.'[17]

The MCC too was very keen to undertake the tour and passed a series of motions supporting the visit. Even the County Cricket Advisory Committee expressed keenness about the tour with a view to encouraging cricket in India.[18]

However, when everything seemed to be going right, the Bombay Hindu Gymkhana announced their decision to not support the tour. Commenting on the move by the Hindu Gymkhana, the *Times of India* declared:

> It is feared that the projected visit of the MCC cricketers to India this coming cold weather will not materialize after all. It was confidently expected that no opposition would be forthcoming from Bombay, as the Board of Control had received favourable replies from all centers of India. The Hindu Gymkhana has, however, refused to cooperate with the Bombay Cricket Association. At a recent meeting of the Association when the proposed tour was discussed, a letter from the Hindu Gymkhana was read in which they stated that they were unable to participate in any of the matches with the MCC. During investigations by a representative of the *Times of India* it was revealed that the Bombay Presidency Cricket Association has written to the Cricket Control Board acquainting them of the facts adding they were unable to give the Board a guarantee of Rs. 20,000, which was asked for.[19]

In another report titled 'What is the truth about the proposed boycott of the MCC cricketers by the Hindus and Parsees of Bombay?' the paper suggested:

> It will be remembered that last year the intended visit of the English team was cancelled on account of the political troubles of the country. It was hoped, however, that this year when another invitation was sent to London, all would be plain sailing and that we in India would have in our midst in the coming cold weather a strong cricket team sponsored by the MCC.
>
> But alas, all is not plain sailing and the probabilities are now that India will have to wait another year and perhaps, two, before she receives a visit from English cricketers. Rumours have been current in Bombay for some time now that all was not well. At a meeting held recently at Bombay of the Bombay Presidency Cricket Association, it was decided that a letter should be sent to the Indian board of Control stating that it would not be advisable for the MCC team to visit Bombay.[20]

The report concluded saying:

It is interesting to note that very favorable replies have been received from all other centers of India, including the Punjab, Madras and Calcutta and it does seem a pity that Bombay should not see its way clear to make the invitation to the MCC unanimous. In addition to the resolutions sent to the Board of Control for Cricket in India by the Bombay committee, it is understood that the Parsee Gymkhana has also sent a letter to the highest authorities stating that it would not be advisable for the MCC to visit Bombay.[21]

Soon after the publication of these reports, the BCCI issued the following statement to the press:

The only cricket Association, which finds itself unable to support the proposed tour is the Bombay Presidency Cricket Association. The Hindu Gymkhana, Bombay, have advised the BCA of their inability to take part in the Association's activities. The Bombay Cricket Association has advised the BCCI that in these circumstances and owing to the very obscure and unsettled local situation, they are unable to approve of an MCC visit to Bombay this cold weather.[22]

The reason assigned by the Hindu Gymkhana for its refusal to cooperate was that the country was facing an uncertain political situation with Gandhi giving a clarion call for civil disobedience against the British and with the participation of the Congress in the Second Round Table Conference being still uncertain. Despite Bombay's opposition, the *Times of India* published the following report:

In response to an invitation from the MCC, Board of Control for Cricket in India patron Lord Willingdon has accepted the suggestion to play for his team against the MCC when the latter visit India next cold weather, provided the fixture does not clash with His Excellency's other arrangements.[23]

Another report published on 15 June 1931 declared:

Except Bombay every center has cordially approved the proposal and will accord the tourists a very hearty welcome. Even in Bombay the general desire is to see the cream of England's cricketers in action on the maidan and it is only the attitude hitherto adopted by the Hindu Gymkhana, which is the one snag in the way of the tour materializing. It rests with the Bombay Hindus to take immediate action and accord the tour their official support and approval. If the Bombay Hindu Gymkhana says that they will welcome the team as sportsmen and leave all other considerations aside, not only would they ensure that the MCC will send the team, but they will be doing Indian cricket inestimable good.[24]

However, in view of the continuing opposition from the Hindu Gymkhana, the MCC was forced to postpone its visit to India, evident from the following announcement in the *Times of India* on 4 July 1931:

> A cable has been received from the MCC to the effect that the committee considered it preferable that the visit proposed for next cold weather be postponed. Their decision is due to the fact that some of the matches originally proposed cannot at present be arranged. They indicated before arranging the tour that they wished to be assured that all the main cricket centers will participate and thus obtain full benefit of the tour. Whilst much regretting having to postpone their visit to India at present the MCC expressed satisfaction and pleasure at the prospect of welcoming an Indian side in England next year.[25]

Soon after the news of postponement was made public, the Hindu Gymkhana withdrew the ban on the tour, lending strength to the conjecture that the earlier policy of the Gymkhana was a clear-cut 'strategy', adopted to thwart the visit. Commenting on the Gymkhana's decision to lift the ban, the *Times of India* said:

> The decision taken by the Hindu Gymkhana at its central meeting held on Sunday (19 July) removing the ban has been acclaimed as a step of wisdom in the sporting world. Interviewed by a representative of the *Times of India*, L.R. Tairsee, the President of the Gymkhana, who played an important part in persuading the Gymkhana to revise its attitude, stated that he was very glad that an unanimously agreed formula has been arrived at and his only regret was that the Hindu Gymkhana had not been approached at an early stage, otherwise, he thought there would be no need to cancel the MCC tour of India.[26]

This narrative demonstrates that the history of cricket in Bombay must take into account the colonial context, read in terms of power equations between the coloniser and the colonised. This is not to say that one can read a straightforward narrative of the rise, spread and flowering of anti-European sentiment into cricket. Existing historiography of cricket in Bombay reads very much like a simple narrative of transposition—where the specificity of sport itself is lost, and might well be replaced with matters like Western education or desire for upward mobility and still make much sense! Such an approach fails to explain why the game has outlived colonialism and has generated the mass following that it has in post-independence India.

2
The Cricketing Jam
Ranji's Leg Glance to the Throne

It is important to keep in mind that had Ranjitsinhji not played English games, he would never have become an Indian prince. He would, in all likelihood, have languished as a minor casualty of the politics of a minor Indian state.[1]

Just as the Parsees did not play cricket simply to be like the British, so too, Ranji, arguably the most debated cricketer in India's cricketing history, was not simply an Anglophile. He was much more—a self-aware individual who used the colonial state to suit his ends, a Nawanagar nationalist and a good uncle to his nephew Duleep. A complex personality who achieved great heights with his cricket, Ranji remains, despite his numerous biographies, an enigma to most scholars of cricket in India.

Ranjitsinhji, ruler of Nawanagar between 1907–33, had a disputed succession. Born in 1872 to a Jadeja family of Sarodar, Ranji had no legal claim to the throne. The Jam, Vibhaji, ruler of Nawanagar, made him heir apparent to the throne after he decided to disinherit his son, Kalubha, on charges of misdemeanour.[2] Kalubha, son of Dhanbai, one of the Jam's Muslim concubines, was disinherited in 1877 on charges of attempting to poison the Jam. Having no other son, Vibhaji adopted Ranji, son of a distant relative, in 1878. Prior to Ranji's adoption, the Jam had adopted Ranji's elder brother, Umedsinhji, as the future heir.[3] When Umedsinhji died within six months of his adoption, the Jam made Ranji the heir apparent.[4] However, when Janbai, sister of Dhanbai, bore the Jam a son in 1882, Ranji's claim to the throne was annulled.[5] Under pressure from members of his zenana, Vibhaji appealed to the British government to accept Jaswantsinhji, the newborn, as the future ruler because he was the Jam's own son. The appeal was accepted and Ranji was disinherited in 1884.[6]

Despite having been disinherited, Ranji did eventually become Jam in 1907. How Ranji became the Jam of Nawanagar is a unique story which has no parallel in the history of cricket in India. A riveting drama, it brings to light the importance attached to cricketing prowess at the turn of the century. This is a story which makes it possible for us to go as far as to assert that Ranji's succession to the throne would have been impossible had he not turned out to be one of the world's best cricketers.

Ranji's cricket skills endeared him to the British administrators of India/Jamnagar and many of them were keen to meet him during his visit to Kathiawar in 1898–99.[7] The following account by Charles Kincaid, Judicial Officer of Jamnagar, bears testimony to Ranji's status as cricketer:

> After the end of Mr. Stoddart's tour (to Australia) Ranjitsinhji paid a visit to Kathiawar. He stayed there for several months, and it was then that I first made his acquaintance. All the agency officials were anxious to meet the famous cricketer; but the situation was rather delicate. The King emperor's representative at Rajkot was pledged to the support of the young Jam Jaswantsinhji. Fortunately as a Judicial Officer I was not so bound. I invited Ranjitsinhji to my house, and he cordially accepted the invitation. I expected to find a young man embittered by the decision of the government of India and his head turned by his cricket success. I found on the contrary, a charming youth, who treated the viceroy's decision as a blow of fate to be endured, rather than to be rallied against, and who spoke of his prodigious cricket scores with the most becoming modesty. I took him as a guest to the officer's mess at Rajkot, and everyone was delighted with him. The Colonel afterwards remarked to me bluntly that he wished all his English guests had as good manners as Ranjitsinhji.[8]

Friendship soon turned into support and many of the administrators wanted Ranjitsinhji to be crowned Jam, well aware, however, that he had no legal claim to the throne. As Kincaid declares:

> In 1903 his (Ranji's) fortunes reached the Nadir. In March of that year, Jaswantsinhji was formally installed as Jam of Jamnagar by the agent of the Governor. He was an unattractive figure. He had had every advantage—an English tutor, education at the Rajkumar College, constant coaching at cricket, tennis, polo, pigsticking, hockey, shooting. Yet, he never learnt to play any game properly. Nor did he ever show the least interest in sport. I, as an agency official, attended the ceremony of installation. I well remember my disgust when I saw this loutish bastard of a lowborn concubine seated on the throne of Jam Rawal; while my unfortunate friend, the lawful heir, had not even been invited to the investiture.[9]

Their unequivocal support for Ranji was evident when, after Jaswant-sinhji's death, the British Resident accepted Ranji's claim to the throne in 1907: 'At last justice prevailed. On 7th March 1907, Ranjitsinhji was installed on the throne of his ancestors to the delight of all save the corrupt clique that had battened on the incompetence of Jaswantsinhji.'[10]

In his struggle for the throne, Ranji also received support from some of the powerful ruling princes, namely, Patiala, Idar and Jodhpur.[11] This support too, as Kincaid asserts, owed much to his cricketing abilities. Even when the British Resident of western India refused to acknowledge his claim, his support base had not dwindled, a just comment on what prowess in cricket meant in colonial India:

> (In 1898) the young prince found the Jamnagar throne barred and bolted against him; so, after some little time, he returned to England. His kinsman, the Maharaja Pratapsinhji of Idar and Jodhpur, the Maharaja of Patiala and many other Indian chiefs helped him, for they were justly proud of his extraordinary success in first class cricket.[12]

With Ranji in dire financial straits at the turn of the century, many ruling princes came forward to help him, wishing to associate with the world's leading cricketer. In 1898, Pratapsinhji appointed Ranji a Sirdar of Jodhpur, an appointment that carried with it an annual grant of Rs. 30,000.[13] He also arranged for Ranji to meet with the Nawab of Patiala, one of the wealthiest men in contemporary India. This meeting, as Simon Wilde declares, proved to be of great significance for Ranji as Rajinder, the Nawab of Patiala, soon 'established himself as Ranji's latest benefactor, probably his most generous to date'.[14] It was as a mark of this friendship that Ranji toured parts of India as a member of the Maharaja's team in 1898–99.[15]

Likewise, British administrators tried to bail Ranji out of his financial difficulties on grounds that it was unworthy of a great cricketer to suffer such ignominy. An officer who did much for Ranji was Lieutenant Colonel Kennedy, the administrator of Nawanagar. Impressed by Ranji's heroism on the cricket field in 1896, when he scored a century on debut for England against Australia, Kennedy tried to double the allowance Ranji received from the treasury. In his letter of 8 November 1897 addressed to his senior, Colonel Hunter, he argued: 'I understand the people at home will only be too glad if Ranji the popular idol of the hour gets plenty.'[16]

Kennedy's letter evoked a favourable response from Lieutenant Colonel John Hunter, the Resident at Rajkot. In his letter to the India Office in London, Colonel Hunter wrote:

> Colonel Kennedy proposes again to double Ranjitsinhji's allowance—which means quadrupling the sum originally stipulated for by the Kumar's father.

There can be no question that this is a very generous provision to which the Kumar has no actual right, but which under the peculiar circumstances of his case may be sanctioned not as a compensation for the Kumar's disappointment at being set aside...but in view of the surrounding's and mode of life into which the young man has been educated, which perhaps render it difficult for him to maintain himself comfortably even on the originally enhanced allowance.[17]

Even when his appeal to win back the *gadi* was dismissed in 1899, Ranji's supporters did not lose hope. The Nawab of Patiala appointed him aide-de-camp (ADC) during the visit of the Viceroy, Lord Elgin, to Patiala giving him an opportunity to present his case to the Viceroy in person. This opportunity proved useful, with the Viceroy ordering that the Government of India wished to see all documentation submitted by Ranji regarding his claim to the throne.[18] Ranji's case was strengthened by Lord Curzon's appointment as Viceroy, chiefly because the latter was a keen cricket follower and an admirer of Ranji. Curzon, having seen Ranji in action for Sussex and England, was expected to treat him favourably.[19]

In 1895, Ranji had accepted an offer from Blackwood and Sons to produce a book, which included chapters on the techniques of playing cricket. The product was the *Jubilee Book of Cricket*, published in 1897. The book was dedicated to the Queen Empress and hailed the Victorian ideal of fair play. In the very next year Ranji spoke of the virtues of 'fair play' to assert that he was the rightful claimant to the throne. He argued that the English who believed in 'fair play' should return the throne to him. In fact in a prayer that he had written as a student at Cambridge, which later became required recitation at English public schools, he hailed the Victorian virtue of fair play thus:

O Powers that be, make me to observe and keep the rules of the game. Help me not to cry for the moon. Help me neither to offer nor to welcome cheap praise. Give me always to be a good comrade. Help me to win, if I may win, but—and this, O Powers, especially—if I may not win, make me a good loser.[20]

When he was touring Australia with Stoddart's team in 1898, Ranji accepted a contract to write a column for the *Australian Review of Reviews*.[21] Finally, when sued by his friend, Mansur Kachar, for non-payment of dues in 1904, Ranji decided to write a book, *Cricket Guide and How to Play Cricket*, published in London in 1906.[22] This book, it is evident from his letters to his love, Mary Holmes, was written with the intention to earn enough to pay back his debts. He had hoped to sell 5,000 copies of the book, claiming in his letter to have secured orders for 3,000 copies, a telling comment on cricket's popularity.[23] Kachar, a childhood friend, lent him Rs. 10,000 hoping that Ranji would use his favourable relations with Curzon to advance Kachar's claims to become Raja of his state. However, Ranji did nothing to this end and Kachar finally sued him for fraud in 1904.[24]

With Jaswantsinhji's death in 1906, Ranji once again had an opportunity to stake his claim to the *gadi*. Of the claimants who presented their cases before the government for consideration, Lakhuba, son of Kalubha, the disinherited son of Jaswantsinhji, and Ranji were the most influential.[25] Though Jaswantsinhji's queens claimed a right to rule, it was quickly brushed aside making it a contest between the two strongest incumbents.[26] Ranji had an advantage over his rival because of his cricketing prowess, which endeared him to the British. Leading British newspapers came out to support Ranji, and, 'on 13 November an unsigned article appeared in *The Times* which argued at length his claim to the Nawanagar throne'.[27]

A comparative analysis of the petitions submitted by both, Ranji and Lakhuba, to the British Resident reflects that Lakhuba's claim to the throne was legal and just. In his petition, submitted to the Governor and President of the Bombay Council, Lakhuba asserted that he was the only surviving descendant of Jam Vibhaji and hence was the rightful heir to the throne.[28] He mentioned that after the recognition of Jaswantsinhji as heir in 1884, Vibhaji had assigned to Lakhuba the status of a 'fataya' meaning 'cadet' or 'heir presumptive' and established him in that position through various rituals and ceremonies.[29] His position entitled him to a *giras* grant of 12 villages. Referring to this grant he asserted:

> It will be seen firstly that it couples the name of Jaswantsinhji with that of the Jam Shri Vibhaji to show that Jaswantsinhji was the heir apparent and successor. Secondly it will be noticed that it styles me Kumar Lakhaji a style appropriate to a fataya or cadet. Thirdly the number of villages granted to me is the number, which a younger son is entitled by the custom of the reigning family of Nawanagar...my grandfather also gave me the very same residence in Nawanagar which had been given to him when he was a fataya. My grandfather also annually celebrated my birthday.... In short in all respects my grandfather treated me as a cadet and presumptive heir since 1885.[30]

He concluded saying that the above facts proved beyond doubt

> ...that it was the fixed determination of my grandfather to establish me in the position of a fataya or heir presumptive, so that I might succeed to the

gadi in the contingency which has now happened, viz, the death of Jaswantsinhji without a male issue and that in that event of Jaswantsinhji leaving
no male issue surviving him, in their default, myself and my male descendants
should succeed to the *gadi*.[31]

His observations about Ranji's petition also point to the validity of his
claims:

Another most important point in connection with Ranjitsinhji's pretensions
is that he was never in fact adopted, the adoption ceremonies having, in his
case, been intentionally omitted by Jam Shri Vibhaji. The latter always
asserted and maintained that although he had obtained the sanction of the
government to adopt Ranjitsinhji he had never in fact adopted him. My
grandfather deliberately refrained from performing the requisite ceremonies.
It appears that in the case of Umedsinhji [Ranji's brother who died prema-
turely] the ceremonies had been performed whereupon he was given a new
name, Raisinhji. The fact that Ranjitsinhji's name was never changed confirms
what Jam Vibhaji used to maintain viz. that he had never in fact adopted
Ranjitsinhji.[32]

Lakhuba summed up his case against Ranji arguing that the adoption
of Ranjitsinhji was illegal:

Firstly, an adoption during the lifetime of a son, grandson or great grandson
is absolutely prohibited by the Hindu law, and is therefore void *ab initio*.
Secondly, it is distinctly opposed to the terms of the sanads of adoption which
permit adoptions only on failure of natural heirs, and that the words 'natural
heirs' cannot, but include a son or a grandson. Thirdly, it is opposed to the
government letter transmitting the sanads, which explicitly states that an
adoption in opposition to family custom will not be recognised. Fourthly,
adoptions are opposed to the custom of all the Rajput principalities of which
Jamnagar is one and of all.... Fifthly, the solitary instance of adoption in
Jamnagar cannot authorise other subsequent departures from a well-known
and firmly established custom, especially when all the attendant circumstances of that case and antecedent history of Jamnagar are taken into
account. Sixthly, Ranjitsinhji was never adopted in fact, that Jam Shri Vibhaji
intentionally refrained from performing ceremonies, and on this account
also the alleged adoption is a mere nullity. Seventhly, a provisional sanction
for adoption subsequently revoked can lend no support whatever to
Ranjitsinhji's pretensions, which have no basis independent of the revoked
sanction.[33]

Though justified, and stronger than Ranji's, Lakhuba's claims were
summarily rejected and the government on 20 February 1907 announced Ranji as Jaswantsinhji's successor to the Nawanagar throne.

Commenting on this decision Wilde declares, 'Of course, Ranji was significantly assisted in his claim by his immense popularity as a cricketer and also by his friendship with the British, perhaps particularly his personal acquaintance with Lord Lamington, the Governor of Bombay.'[34]

After becoming Jam Saheb, Ranji used cricket to further the cause of his state. By the time of his accession, his skills at the game were on the wane. However, he returned to Sussex to play after the First World War, in 1920.[35] He had lost an eye during the war making it doubly difficult for him to play as before. Rather than trying to demonstrate his skills at the game, Ranji used his name to win concessions for his state. Harbouring an ambition of making his state a leading princely power, Ranji set about this task in England. Given its size, Nawanagar could not enjoy the status that princely states like Baroda or Patiala did. Ranji capitalised on his fame as a cricketer, convincing the Secretary of State for India, Lord Montague, to grant Nawanagar the status of a princely state. King George's visit to Nawanagar improved his chances, raising Nawanagar to the status of a leading princely state. As Mihir Bose declares, 'Ranji knew how well cricket and diplomacy could be made to work.'[36]

That cricket was for Ranji the trump card that won him the *gadi* and concessions for his native Nawanagar, makes room for the contention that the charge that Ranji was an Anglophile, and had no interest in Indian cricket, is unfounded. Most Indian cricket administrators who felt betrayed by his nonchalance towards the development of Indian cricket levelled this charge at him, a charge accepted in most existing works on Indian cricket: 'Ranji did absolutely nothing for Indian sport and sportsmen. To all our requests for aid, encouragement and advice, Ranji gave but one answer: Duleep (his nephew) and I are English cricketers. Ranji could not have been more blunt.'[37] His opposition to the nationalist agenda, spearheaded by the Indian National Congress, further intensified the charge.

However, it has to be said that his opposition to nationalism was driven by selfish considerations, and to that extent Ranji's anti-nationalism was a stance projected to achieve his ambitions. He looked upon the Congress move to boycott British goods as an opportunity to boost Nawanagar trade.[38] The anti-British campaign had a disastrous consequence for ports like Bombay, and Ranji made the most of the opportunity to improve the economic condition of his ailing state, and spent a huge amount in developing the port of Bedi.[39] On his last visit to England in 1932, Ranji publicised this economic advance, giving details of Nawanagar's profits. Addressing a meeting arranged by the

Manchester Chamber of Commerce, and keen to increase the volume of trade with India, he asserted, 'Over the last two or three years we in my state have trebled, if not quadrupled, the sale of Manchester goods because we felt that Bombay's stupidity was our opportunity.'[40]

At the same time, the text of a speech delivered at the 1922 session of the League of Nations raises doubts regarding the charge that Ranji was an Anglophile unconcerned with the fortunes of his countrymen. On this occasion, he spoke against restrictions on the immigration of Indians to the colonies and criticised the empire's policy in South Africa:

> I should feel false to my fellow countrymen in India, and also to my fellow countrymen in South Africa, were I to neglect this unique opportunity of summoning to the assistance of their aspirations the spiritual power and the spiritual blessing of your sympathy.... What is our ideal? What is our purpose? What is the very reason of our being? Let us have catholic justice and we shall have catholic peace.[41]

His speech provoked enormous displeasure among representatives from Australia and South Africa. He was also critical of the British government's efforts to set up a federation in India and fell out with Lord Willingdon on this issue. Using cricketing metaphors for the umpteenth time in his life, 'The princes of India have been very old members of Great Britain's team and they have tried their best to play with a straight bat for the empire', Ranji demanded complete immunity from supervision by a federal government.[42]

His refusal to allow Duleep to play for India, arguing that he was an English cricketer, may be explained in terms of the benefits on offer for cricketers in England. Having played for England himself, Ranji was aware that Duleep could earn a better living by playing for England. Though there was no match fee for amateurs in England, he could make money from writing books on cricket and from receiving donations and gifts, which he would invariably receive if he excelled as an English cricketer. With such opportunities still a rarity in India, he was opposed to Duleep representing the home country.

Finally, as Cashman asserts, Ranji did assist in the development of Indian cricket in ways that often pass unnoticed. To him goes the credit of spotting Ladha Amar Singh, one of India's outstanding cricketers of the 1930s. He also shared cricket coaches, hired to train players of the Nawanagar team with other states, and captained the state team on many occasions.[43] He promoted cricket in Nawanagar in an effort to attract the English monarch to his state, a strategy that proved successful.

It was only because of cricket that Ranji could earn the following eulogy:

> O Statesmen, who devise and plot,
> To keep the white above the black;
> Who tremble when your bolt is shot
> Lest love and loyalty grow slack.
> There's not a deed of craftsmanship,
> There's not a thing Red tape can do,
> Shall knit the Hindoo to the Celt
> As much as this—the Cambridge Blue!
>
> No million acres of Dispatch,
> No tanks of governmental ink
> Can force a native not to watch
> For days when England's star may sink.
> Build factories to weave the tape,
> Make tables for the rice and dew;
> Do all your best, and you shall miss
> The binding force of Cambridge blue!
>
> An Indian gentleman to-day
> Has staled your tortoise policy;
> And thousand cheer to see him play,
> A splendid batsman quick and free.
> A game shall dwindle all your cares,
> A clever catch and runs a few.
> A Parliament may fool indeed,
> But not the band of Cambridge Blue![44]

3

Birthpangs
Naming the Ranji Trophy

Cricket, as we have seen in the previous chapter, gave Ranji his royal seat. Cricket as we will see in this chapter, gave him immortality as well. The Ranji Trophy continues even today to be the premier cricket tournament at the national level in India, but how it came into being is a sensational story now almost forgotten.

This is a story with princely intrigue, rivalries, twists and turns, and a dramatic finale. On a deeper level, it demonstrates how princes and zamindars used cricket as a ladder for social mobility to compensate for their waning influence in matters of state. There were numerous sub-plots in this story, but the central characters were only two: the Maharaja of Patiala[1] and the Maharajkumar of Vizianagram, better known as Vizzy, not a ruling prince but enthusiastic and determined to establish his eminence through cricket.

By the early 1930s, the Maharaja of Patiala was among the most powerful princes in India and controlled the activities of the newly formed Board of Control for cricket.[2] He had donated huge amounts towards the building of the Cricket Club of India[3] and was the vice-patron of the Board, second only to Lord Willingdon who was the patron by virtue of being the Viceroy. Patiala employed senior cricketers and supported Ranjitsinhji in times of financial crisis, as evident in Chapter 2. However, it was beginning to be clear by the early 1930s that the Maharaja of Patiala was fast falling out of favour with Lord Willingdon, as a result of the former's involvement in numerous sexual scandals—written about in a book, *Indictment of Patiala*, authored by one of the Maharaja's own subjects. Thus, the situation was ripe for the emergence of a new player in Indian cricket.

The challenger was the Maharajkumar of Vizinanagram, who, though he hailed from a South Indian princely state, had settled in Benaras following a quarrel with his nephew. He rose to prominence in 1930 by organising a tour to Ceylon and other parts of India.

The political situation in India in 1930 was one of turmoil. Mahatma Gandhi had launched the Civil Disobedience Movement against the British, which resulted in the cancellation of the proposed MCC tour, as we have seen in Chapter 1. Vizzy capitalised on this opportunity by forming a team to tour parts of India and Ceylon. This team included, among others, Jack Hobbes and Herbert Sutcliffe, two living legends of English cricket,[4] along with prominent Indian players like C.K. Nayudu, Mushtaq Ali and D.B. Deodhar.[5] This tour catapulted Vizzy into a position of power as a leading figure of Indian cricket, a position strengthened by the praise showered on him by Sutcliffe. Commenting on the tour in the *Daily Express*, Sutcliffe declared,

> The Maharajkumar is a candidate for the captaincy for the Indian team to tour England, and if he is fortunate enough to be appointed, he will no doubt give an excellent account of himself for he has had a thorough grounding in the finer points of the game, and is a most capable leader.[6]

Vizzy used this newfound success to project himself as a rival to the Maharaja of Patiala. This is evident from the following report published in the *Times of India*:

The Indian Cricket Tour

Magnificent offer by the Maharajkumar of Vizianagram Towards Expenses

Nawab Liaqat Ali Khan, the retiring President of the Cricket Control Board interviewed by a press representative at Delhi station enroute to Bombay for the Round Table Conference made the following statement: The emergency meeting of the All India Cricket Board was hurriedly convened at Simla in view of his departure last week to consider three important questions 1. Appointment of Officers, 2. The proposed tour to England, 3. The visit of the Ceylon team to India next winter.

He was glad to say that he was in receipt of an offer to contribute rupees 50,000 from the Maharaj Kumar (of Vizianagram), which was welcomed by the Board. Mr. De Mello, who was also present, said, he had wired the Maharaj Kumar to get to Delhi as early as possible to meet the Board to discuss financial matters when Mr. C.E. Newham, the acting President and Mr. R.E. Grant Govan, will be in Delhi.[7]

In an interview with the Associated Press soon after his arrival in Delhi, Vizzy declared:

He had undertaken the journey only for the sake of cricket. He had come to Delhi to meet the officials of Board of Control and was going to make every endeavour for the materialisation of the cricket tour to England. The cancellation of the MCC visit to India was to him and doubtless to all lovers of cricket in India a great shock, and he was therefore prepared to make any sacrifice, financial or otherwise, to help towards the tour to England.[8]

The report went on to state that:

He now notices a distinct involvement in Southern India after the tour he made last winter with Hobbes and Sutcliffe and he had no doubt whatsoever that cricket in India would benefit with a side from India visiting England. After the long tour he completed last year visiting Benares, Delhi, Calcutta, Madras, Bangalore, Secundrabad and Ceylon, he felt sure there was able cricket talent in India and both the renowned English cricketers, Hobbes and Sutcliffe, felt exactly the same.[9]

After the meeting in Delhi, the following report was published in the *Times of India*:

No Financial Anxiety

An important statement made after the meeting of the emergency committee held in Delhi on Friday was that all anxiety regarding the financial side of the tour had vanished as a result of the generosity of the Maharajkumar of Vizianagram who had written a letter to the Board marking a donation of rupees 50,000 to the Board of which 40,000 must be earmarked for the tour to England next year. The position now is that the Vizianagram donation should ensure a surplus for the benefit of Indian cricket.[10]

The correspondent concluded saying, 'I understand the Maharajkumar of Vizianagram will captain the Indian team (to England) next year.'[11]

Soon after this meeting Vizzy met the Viceroy, Lord Willingdon, to discuss arrangements for the forthcoming English tour on 27 November 1931. This meeting, reported widely in the national press, was touted as a major success:

The Maharajkumar of Vizianangram who is here in connection with the meeting of the Board of Control interviewed and discussed with the Viceroy the proposed tour of the Indian cricket XI to England. His Excellency, it is understood, evinced keen interest in Indian cricket, especially with regard to the forthcoming visit of an Indian XI to England next year.[12]

The struggle for supremacy between Vizzy and Patiala was thus out in the open before the 1932 tour of England. With Vizzy having won the first round, the Maharaja of Patiala came back to win the second by agreeing to sponsor the trials of the touring party. In the annual general meeting of the Board in November 1931, Patiala announced his intention to sponsor the trials, agreeing alongside to take care of the finances of the touring party for a whole month.[13] This offer was too tempting for the financially impoverished Board to refuse,[14] enabling the Nawab to reinforce his supremacy over Indian cricket.[15]

That both princes were vying for the captaincy of the touring team became apparent when cricketers from around the country started taking sides on the issue. In a letter addressed to the Editor of the *Times of India*, an Indian cricketer of the past asserted:

> In the first place there was a report in the Statesman of Delhi some days ago that the Nawab of Pataudi had intimated his willingness to forego his qualification for Worcestershire county if he was selected to play for India. Of his selection of course, there is no doubt. Even with that case, with all due respect to the Nawab, he is far from an ideal skipper for the Indian team, as he would be lacking the necessary knowledge of the abilities of the men under his command, a necessity with which your correspondent agrees. In my opinion the Maharaj Kumar of Vizianagram is obviously the best choice, and I put the Nawab of Pataudi with his extensive knowledge of the conditions in England as the second in charge.[16]

Within a couple of days of the publication of this letter, M.E. Pavri, the famous Parsee stalwart, wrote a letter to the Editor which went as follows:

> Sir, I quite agree with the 'Indian Cricketer' from Karachi who had written a letter in the Times of India except about the captaincy. I beg to differ from him entirely on this question about appointing the Maharajkumar of Vizianagram in preference to the Nawab of Pataudi, who with his vast experience of English cricket conditions and with the opportunity that he will get of playing with the members of the team and so getting to know them during the trial matches and practice games, would be the ideal captain in the absence of Prince Duleepsinhji. The great sporting enthusiast, the Maharaja of Patiala, however, would be the most appropriate skipper, if His Highness can make up his mind to play all the matches in England.[17]

However, it was the hosting of the trials during 23–29 January 1932 that tilted the issue in Patiala's favour and he was appointed captain of the touring party on 4 February 1932.[18] That this was the most likely outcome was already mentioned in the *Times of India*:

> A popular item of discussion in cricket circles across the country is the official announcement of the selection, which takes place in the evening of February

4. The selection committee will meet at Montgomery Hall at 3.30 p.m. tomorrow and submit their recommendation to the Board of Control who will then select a captain, a vice-captain and a deputy vice captain. Rumours are that the Maharaja of Patiala will skipper the All India side and the two other places are being filled by the Maharajkumar of Vizianagram and K.S. Ghanshyamsinhji, though their respective roles are not known.[19]

Patiala's election evoked mixed responses in the media. This is borne out by the publication of two contrasting reports in the *Times of India* on 6 February 1932. The first described the selection of the Maharaja of Patiala as a 'tribute to His Highness['s] long and devoted service to the cause of Indian cricket'.[20] The second, by contrast, declared, 'the selection of the Maharaja of Patiala as captain of the team is, however, a strange nomination, as it can hardly be claimed that he merits a place in the team on form alone. Neither can his tactical knowledge be considered very high.'[21] It went on to suggest that, 'it is very likely that he will be a non-playing captain and that Prince Ghanshyamsinhji will be skipper on the field itself.'[22] The report concluded saying that 'his Highness, the Maharaja of Patiala will undoubtedly be in his element in the social side of the tour and this is probably the reason for his official nomination as captain.'[23]

Vizzy, the defeated challenger, who was given the subordinate position of deputy vice-captain, withdrew from the tour citing personal reasons and worked on cosying up to Lord Willingdon. Saying that he was 'broken hearted' Vizzy issued the following statement:

> I have just sent a letter to the President of the Board of Control for Cricket in India and I can hardly express how broken hearted I am, but I am making this immense sacrifice for the future of cricket in India, for which I worked so hard for the past two years, and shall continue to do so in the future. The Board of Control have indeed bestowed on me a very great honour by appointing me Deputy Vice-Captain of the team that is to tour England next summer. I not only regret, but am very disappointed that I shall not be able to undertake this tour.
>
> I have not been well for the greater part of the current cricket season, and this has been responsible for my very bad form throughout and loving the game of cricket as I do, I keenly feel that I shall not be able to do justice to your selection and to the team if my present form continues and I fear that this will be so with my confidence so shaken after my recent performances.[24]

Arguing that a position in the team was a 'coveted one', Vizzy went on to assert:

As you are aware my efforts combined with those of the Board from September last have led to the materialisation of the visit to England and while I feel my recent continued bad performances doubtless deprived me of the captaincy of the tour, for which till not so very long ago I was considered fit and practically a certainty. I feel that on the success of the present tour depends to a very large extent India's future in international cricket and I shall therefore, be obliged if you will appreciate for the sake of the future of India's cricket I am sacrificing my coveted position in the side.[25]

In the wake of Vizzy's statement, the Maharaja of Patiala announced his decision not to tour, reported in the *Times of India* of 3 March 1932:

The Board of Control for Cricket in India have now received confirmation from His Highness the Maharaja of Patiala that he much regrets his inability to accept the captaincy of the cricket team to tour England this summer as he finds that it will not be possible for him to get away.[26]

In conveying this decision, Patiala thanked the Board for inviting him to lead the team and said that had he found 'it possible to accept the invitation nothing would have given him greater pleasure than to lead the team'.[27]

Finally, the Maharaja of Porbander was appointed captain of the touring team on 15 March 1932. Vizzy greeted his appointment in the following words:

On the eve of my departure to Europe, I feel I must offer my felicitations to the Indian team under the Maharaja of Porbander sailing early next month. I have had the hand in the formation of the side and I am proud to say that it constitutes the core and kernel of cricket talent in India. I shall watch its career in the West with deepest interest. I wish them the very best of success, and hope that they will prove the true representative of India, both on the field and away from it.[28]

Perhaps the worst player of the touring party, Porbander soon realised his lack of skill and was content to leave the captaincy to C.K. Nayudu, arguably the best player of the side.[29] Vizzy made use of Nayudu's rise and his growing unpopularity within the team to plot against Patiala. He deliberately sang praises of Nayudu, who, by the end of the tour, was greatly unpopular among his teammates, who in turn, reports indicate, were already unhappy with his autocratic attitude.[30] The side that was initially united under Patiala's leadership was deeply divided by the end of the tour. Soon after the tour was over, Vizzy donated a pavilion at the newly built Feroze Shah Kotla stadium in Delhi naming it after Lord Willingdon.[31] These efforts to curry favour with the Viceroy were successful, and though Patiala was elected Chancellor of the Chamber of Princes after Ranji's death in 1933, his influence over Indian cricket, as Mihir Bose writes in the *History of Indian Cricket*, was declining:

> Willingdon's hostility to Patiala had coincided with the waning of the latter's cricket power. He had been the kingmaker of the 1932 tour, but in the winter of 1933–34 he was pushed to the sidelines. The emergency Board of Control meeting in Delhi on 1 May 1933 showed that the associations, which had once survived because of his generosity were now turning against him.[32]

Patiala, however, had not resigned to the situation and was determined to make a comeback. He once again resorted to his trusted weapon—patronage. He entertained the MCC team lavishly when they toured India in the winter of 1933. Overwhelmed on seeing the grand stadium he had built at Amritsar, they showered generous praise on Patiala; and it was at Patiala that the MCC played the only four-day first-class fixture of the tour. During this match, they were taken for shoots in the hills,[33] and even Jardine, the captain of the touring team, was won over.[34] However, despite his success in reinforcing control over the game, Nayudu was retained as captain for the Test matches against the MCC, overriding the Yuvraj of Patiala, an able cricketer and the son the Maharaja was trying to promote. Vizzy welcomed Nayudu's appointment, whose failure as captain was to pave the way for his rise in the hierarchy. Also, Vizzy utilised the tour to good effect by leading his side to a significant victory against the MCC. This was the MCC's only loss on the tour and it may well have been the result of complacency. Whatever the reason, Douglas Jardine, the MCC captain, did Vizzy's cause a lot of good by proclaiming that he had the potential to be a good skipper. By the end of the MCC tour, therefore, the stage was set for a showdown between the two rival princes. Patiala had an advantage because the game was once again confronted with a financial crisis and Patiala, given his economic position, was the only person capable of solving it, playing the role of benefactor to perfection in the process.

With the Bombay Pentangular tournament stopped for the time being, the time was ripe for a national championship. Commenting on the occasion of the Indian team's return to Bombay from England in 1932, the Mayor of Bombay had emphasised the need for such a championship, claiming that it would do much to strengthen the foundation of the game.[35] Also, with the Board of Control for Cricket in India set up in 1928, the start of a zonal competition was imminent.

Accordingly, at a meeting of the Board in Simla in the summer of 1934, A.S. De Mello, the secretary, stressed the need for a national championship and submitted his proposal for it. He also presented a drawing of the proposed trophy, which Vasant Raiji describes as, 'a Grecian urn two feet high, with a lid, the handle of which represented Father Time, similar to the one on the weather vane at Lords'.[36] As soon as De Mello mooted the plan, the Maharaja of Patiala stood up to declare that he would be pleased to donate the trophy and committed a donation of £500 (Rs. 6,667) at the prevailing exchange rate. He wanted the trophy to be named after Ranji, to honour Ranji's services to the game. The Maharaja also declared his intention to present a miniature trophy to the winners of the championship, one that they could prematurely retain. His offer drew considerable applause.

The connection between Ranji and Patiala was well known. Ranji had played for Patiala's team in 1898–99. While touring Bengal in 1899, Ranji and Patiala had been accorded a royal reception with the Calcutta Town Hall spending the huge sum of Rs. 3,000 on the occasion.

However, as Raiji states, 'For some unknown reason, the official announcement of the decision to launch the Ranji Trophy was withheld.'[37] This allowed Vizzy to work his manipulations at the highest levels. He floated the proposal that the trophy should be named after Lord Willingdon instead of Ranji who, he argued, had done little for the game in India. An emergency meeting of the Board was summoned to discuss the renaming and Vizzy strengthened his case by donating a trophy himself. At this meeting attended by Sir Sikandar Hayat Khan, Liaqat Khan, Vizzy, Patiala, Board President Grant-Govan and A.S. De Mello, the Board accepted the Willingdon Trophy as the national championship of India. Reporting the matter, the *Times of India* declared that the Willingdon Trophy, specially selected by Lady Willingdon, had been gratefully accepted and placed on display. It is worth noting that despite being present at the meeting, Patiala could not prevent the Willingdon Trophy from being accepted.[38]

The rivalry between the two patrons came to a head when their teams met at the final of the Moin-ud-dowlah Trophy in Hyderabad.[39] The match had assumed great significance with both princes determined to stamp their supremacy on the game:

> The two princes had scoured the land for the best cricketers and Vizzy had also obtained Learie Constantine. The teams met in the final and a record crowd of 15,000 turned up at Secundrabad Gymkhana to watch it. Vizzy himself did not take part, a very minor prince, the Rajkumar of Alirajpur, deputised for him. In the middle of the final he sent Constantine a telegram

promising him a certain number of pounds for every run scored and every wicket taken.[40]

Despite all his efforts, Vizzy's side lost by three wickets.

In the meantime, in the aftermath of the acceptance of the Willingdon Trophy by the Board, many newspapers such as the *Bombay Chronicle*, *Star of India* and *Anandabazar Patrika* wrote in support of the Ranji Trophy. For instance, writing in the *Bombay Chronicle*, J.C. Maitra stated:

> I wonder if by doing so [accepting the Willingdon Trophy] they ever thought of the sacrilege they were doing to the memory of the greatest cricketer ever born in India, whose memory is still cherished by thousands of followers of the game in all parts of the world. If such a move is made, the duty of all cricketers in this country is clear. They should rise in a body and oppose the sacrilege.[41]

Despite such protests, it was expected that Bombay, the winners of the first national championship held on their home territory in March 1935, would be presented the Willingdon Trophy.[42] However, a surprise awaited H.J. Vajifdar (who was standing in for the indisposed captain L.P. Jai) when he walked up to collect the trophy a week after the final at an exhibition match against the Cricket Club of India at Delhi. Lord Willingdon was present at the podium to give away the prize, but the trophy he handed out was the Ranji Trophy!

It turned out that Patiala had successfully outmanoeuvred Vizzy while touring England with Grant-Govan in January 1935. The two had represented India at the International Cricket Council (ICC) meeting held at Lords, and it was during this trip that Patiala turned the tables on Vizzy. The trump card was his promise to sponsor Jack Ryder's Australians, who were to tour India in October 1935. To Vizzy's dismay, the Willingdon Trophy was later presented to the winners of the Festival Cup played in Delhi.

However, the fight between the two princes was still not over. Vizzy had the last laugh when he was appointed captain of the Indian team that toured England in May–June 1936. This series saw the sending back of Lala Amarnath, the best performer on the tour, on grounds of indiscipline, a controversy explored in the next chapter.

4

The Amarnath Affair

I have the full authority to announce that a sensational decision to send Amarnath back has been made. He is aboard the Kaiser-I-Hind, which leaves Southampton today.

> Cricket Correspondent E.H.D. Sewell in the *Times of India*.[1]

One of Indian cricket's best known controversies, the Amarnath–Vizzy affair is evidence of the deep-rooted patrician–plebeian divide that plagued cricket in colonial India. A tussle that dragged on after the conclusion of the 1936 tour, this much reported story of intrigue, corruption and power play had enough in it to be a bestseller.

The root of this drama dates back to early 1936, a time when Vizzy was at his diplomatic best, determined to captain the touring team to England that summer. His rival for the captaincy was C.K. Nayudu, Indian cricket's first superstar. That Vizzy had spared no pains to win this election is evident from the following description. 'He had journeyed up and down the country gathering votes. Associations that voted for him were promised special consideration when it came to the choice of players for the tour.'[2]

Vizzy eventually won the coveted prize defeating Nayudu 10–4 in the contest. While Delhi, Bengal, Central Provinces, Maharashtra, United Provinces, Hyderabad, Rajputana, Mysore, Bangalore and Madras voted for Vizzy, Southern Punjab, Northern India, Sind and Bombay voted against him. Central India and Gujarat did not vote and the western Indian states were not present.[3] However, victory in the election was not enough and Vizzy, who hated Nayudu, was intent on isolating him even before the tour commenced.

Soon after the start of the tour Vizzy ordered Lala Amarnath to stay away from Nayudu if he wanted to keep his captain happy. In the words of Amarnath:

While we were at our hotel prior to our match with Oxford University on May 6 the captain's servant came to call me and I went to the captain who straightaway asked me to join his side and not to mix with major C.K. Nayudu and several others with whom I generally mixed. Up to this time I was not aware of any party feelings among the players. Our party consisted of C.K. Nayudu, Gopalan, Mushtaq Ali, Ramaswamy and myself. We generally gathered together. I told the captain that C.K. was a friend of mine, but I was not concerned with any particular party except that we generally went out together. I agreed to do what the captain thought best.[4]

Because Amarnath had duly obliged his captain, Nayudu, in disgust, stopped talking to him.[5] Vizzy, on the other hand, was pleased and congratulated Amarnath for his century at Northamptonshire, and from then on gave him regular rides to the grounds in his car.[6]

The matter should have ended there, but it did not. A confrontation between Vizzy and Amarnath, the best performer of the team, was triggered during the match against Leicester (20–22 May). Amarnath, bowling from the pavilion end, asked the captain to remove the third man and place the fielder between cover and point instead. In response, Vizzy snubbed Amarnath, asking him not to waste time and ordered him to carry on. 'I kept on bowling and was changed after two overs. I then fielded in the country.' After the game, Amarnath made the cardinal mistake of discussing the incident with his mates, saying that he had never seen a captain refuse to assist his bowler so curtly.

News of this got to Vizzy who called Amarnath aside and informed him that as captain he could do whatever he liked.[7] When Amarnath retorted that that did not include the right to insult colleagues, Vizzy brought the incident to the notice of the manager, Major Brittain Jones who ordered Amarnath to apologise. Lala did so as Brittain Jones had promised to help him secure a professional contract to play in the Lancashire league. Vizzy, however, was not satisfied, and in the match against Middlesex at Lord's, Amarnath was asked to field in the deep and was underbowled even though he had taken 6 wickets for 29 runs:

> While playing against Middlesex at Lords (May 23, 25, 26) I was kept in the country all the time and put on to bowl fourth change. Whenever I was put on I took a wicket and was taken off. My analysis in that match was 6 wickets for 29 runs.[8]

Amarnath answered this humiliation with centuries in both innings of the following match against Essex at Brentwood batting at number three. Vizzy congratulated him but was quick to add that had Amarnath not foolishly tried to score off every ball, he could have scored many more runs. In this match, as Amarnath stated, 'I hurt my shin very badly and had to retire for 15 minutes and then took the field after putting on plaster. I fielded wherever I was placed.'[9]

Before the next match against Cambridge University (30 May–2 June), Amarnath sprained his back at the nets. 'The pain was so severe that I cried in agony and was frightened that something serious might have happened,'[10] he recalled later. But the manager ordered him to play ignoring his plea for a much-needed rest. Amarnath went in to bat 10 minutes before lunch and was out leg-before-wicket first ball. When India fielded, he was brought on to bowl first change and hurt himself again. 'I informed the captain and he told me to go to the pavilion. He also went with me and spoke to the manager. I put on my coat and stayed on to watch the match.'[11] After an hour's rest, Brittain Jones brought in a doctor who plastered Amarnath's back. Soon after, Amarnath was ordered into the ground and was asked to tell Vizzy that he could bowl and field:

> I went to the field and gave the chit to the captain and told him that the manager had asked me to say that I could field and bowl. The captain said it was his own look out. After 45 minutes he put me on to bowl and after bowling four or five overs the pain increased considerably and was unbearable. I went in the country to field and came back to bowl again.[12]

At lunch Amarnath had a chat with teammates Amir Elahi,[13] Baqa Jilani[14] and others in Punjabi. Apprehensive of what he was saying, Brittain Jones summoned him for a meeting. 'He had in his hand two letters, one addressed to the Nawab of Bhopal and the other to the Maharaja of Patiala,' Amarnath later remembered.

> These he exhibited threateningly to me, saying that he would post them and also that he would send me back to India as my behaviour was not proper and my language foul. It was obvious that these letters contained some complaints about me. I said that if the manager wanted to send me back to India he could do so as he had the power and I could be sent off the next day.'[15]

However, Brittain Jones informed Lala that he wanted to give him another chance. When Lala retorted that he had not offended anyone and that there was no reason to beg for another chance, Brittain Jones accused him of presuming that he was indispensable and reminded him that he was not.

Amarnath's shin and back had not healed in time for the next match against Yorkshire, but the manager insisted that he should play. In this match too, Amarnath was posted in the deep and had to do much running, aggravating his injury in the process.[16]

The already strained relationship deteriorated further when the manager accused Amarnath of being a womaniser. Amarnath refuted the charge arguing:

> Since I had arrived in England I was always in bed by about 10.30 p.m. on match days and the latest by 11.30 p.m. on off days and I gave no occasion for any one to reprimand me for late nights. I had gone to England to play cricket, which I liked much more than women. He could not have seen me behaving disgracefully or in a compromising way on any occasion and he was not in a position to make any such remark.[17]

This episode was followed by a week-long truce during which Brittain Jones repeatedly emphasised to Amarnath the need to befriend Vizzy. In response, Amarnath informed his manager:

> I have nothing against the captain and said that the captain should not make unkind remarks about me to others. If he was displeased with me in any way he should speak to me directly. I said that I would welcome a reprimand and scolding direct from the captain and manager or even from senior members of the team because I realised the spirit of such an attitude but I was always grieved when I heard outsiders remarking that I was always treading on the corns of those in authority and wilfully getting into their bad books.[18]

Things came to a head during the match against the Minor Counties, which started on 17 June. Amarnath was told he would be batting at number four. However, it was Amar Singh who was eventually sent in at that position. When Amarnath asked Vizzy when he was to go in, he was informed that Vizzy had not yet made up his mind.

Amarnath was finally sent in at number seven, 10 minutes before the end of the day's play.

> In the meantime when one of the players asked the captain why I had been sent in so late he replied that he wanted faster scorers. I played out time and came back to the pavilion rather excited and while undressing threw my pads etc. near my bag in the corner. I felt quite disgusted and talked to several players in Punjabi. What I said was slang, words to the effect that I had not wasted four years uselessly but had learnt cricket.

When Vizzy asked Amarnath whether he was speaking to him, Amarnath insisted that he was not speaking to anyone in particular, nor did he wish to speak to anyone.[19]

After the match, Amar Singh suggested to Amarnath that he should apologise to the captain for his behaviour in the dressing room and that he should do so in writing. He refused to do so saying that he had done nothing to offend his captain for which he needed to send a written apology. Soon after Brittain Jones asked Amarnath to see him at 6 p.m. During this meeting the manager produced a statement signed by several players testifying to Amarnath's misbehaviour. He informed Amarnath that he had decided to send him back to India after a week. An hour later, when Amarnath was in Wazir Ali's room, Brittain Jones came to see him and ordered him to leave by the ship, the *Kaiser-I-Hind*, the very next day. Amarnath begged for another chance but Brittain Jones was adamant. Later that evening, many of the players, Cota Ramaswami, Wazir Ali, Nayudu, Elahi and Dattaram Hindlekar went to the captain and pleaded with him to reconsider the decision. Vizzy gave in on the condition that Amarnath would tender an unqualified written apology. This Amarnath did at once. It was then decided that Vizzy would meet Amarnath the following morning at 8.00 to give the final verdict:

> The next day the captain and I went to the manager's room, but I did not go in. The captain came out in a few minutes and asked me to go to Wazir Ali's room and wait. A little later Wazir Ali came in to inform me that the manager's decision could not be changed and brought back my written guarantee of good behavior. I left by the *Kaiser-I-Hind*.[20]

Commenting on Amarnath's repatriation, the *Times of India* of 20 June 1936 declared:

> It is confirmed that Amarnath is leaving for India this afternoon. The manager of the team, interviewed by Reuter said that Amarnath has been sent back as a disciplinary measure. The matter now rests with the Indian Board of Control and neither the manager nor the captain of the team would make any statement. It appears that Amarnath was warned several times for insolence to his captain and manager, and when reproved for his behaviour off the field he is reported to have said that no action would be taken against him, as he was indispensable to the team. After a lengthy meeting it was decided to teach him a lesson.
>
> Amarnath dismally sitting in a reserved compartment of the boat train at Waterloo told a bitter story to the *Star's* correspondent. He said, 'I am supposed to have been insolent and insubordinate. I did not mean to be rude. This is the end of the trouble that has been going on for some time. It reached a climax at Lords. I did not like the way I was put on to bat. I had played hard, and was tired and flung down the pads. I told the captain that I could not play his way. Last night there was a conference between the manager and the captain who decided to send me away. All my team members have signed a document agreeing that I have been insolent. I do not think all the players are against me. There are a lot of reasons of an extremely private

nature for their agreeing to my being sent away.... I do not mind returning to India, but what will people think of me. I wanted to do my best for the team.'[21]

However, a couple of days after he was sent back, Mushtaq Ali, in an article published in the *Times of India* stood by the manager and the captain. This article published on 23 June went thus:

I went home from Lords last Friday hoping against hope that some way might be found out of the great difficulty wherein the captain and the manager of the Indian team had been placed by Amarnath's behaviour on Thursday evening. I feared the worst as Prince Victor of Cooch Behar had been in the dressing room when the incidents complained of took place, and I felt that the powerful evidence of a non-member of the team, which I knew had been given in support of the Captain and Manager, was likely to clinch matters. Next morning at the Oval I was told the verdict in simple words, 'He will be soon on the boat for India' and I knew that the most sensational happening in the history of cricket tours had taken place. Since then I have become aware of facts, which left me no option but to agree with the drastic decision. The correctness of the decision, severe though some who do not know the facts may think it, was confirmed if the alleged interview (referred above) given by Amarnath in the train was actually given. In that he is alleged to have said that he did say something to other members of the team though not to the captain; and that he had asked to be given another chance.'[22]

Ali reported that Amarnath had been cautioned by the manager before and had apologised to the captain at Leicester agreeing to obey him on the field, though not off it, 'a thoroughly insubordinate remark in itself'.[23] The whole affair, he lamented, was a

sad thing. Certainly it is not the fault of the captain or the manager that this has happened. I hold no brief for either and have freely criticized the captain's decision more than once. But on this occasion, both must and will have the sympathy and the support of every sportsman who understands what cricket means, and that without discipline there can be no cricket.[24]

He concluded saying:

The yarns about dissensions in the team are generally speaking nonsense. Tiffs there always have been and always will be in every touring team. But the cable received here from Bombay, after Amarnath's dismissal, that owing to that, another member of the team was unavailable for the coming Test match is sheer invention. If Amarsingh is meant in this connection the latest news I have is that he has arrived in London today as previously arranged to be in time for the various functions prior to the Test match as well as for the Test. There has never been a hint that Amarsingh will not play in the Test.

The general accusation that there is, or has been, a lot of dissension in the team has no basis in fact.... Everybody is confident that with the Ruler of Bhopal, as President of the Board of Control, Amarnath will get a fair deal. At that, for the time being, this sad case must be permitted to rest.[25]

Back home, Amarnath was whisked away from the Bombay port soon after arrival and was not allowed to speak to the media. He was informed of the Board's decision that he was to go to Bhopal immediately to see the Nawab of Bhopal, the Board President. Following this meeting, the *Times of India* of 15 July reported that:

...the Indian Test player, Amarnath, is returning to England immediately, honourably forgiven and reinstated as a member of the Indian cricket team. He will land at the Croydon aerodrome on Thursday, July 23, and may play in the second Test match at Manchester on July 25–28.[26]

This decision, it was reported, was made by the Nawab of Bhopal after reading the lengthy statement given by Amarnath and after meeting him in person. Following this meeting, the Nawab had instructed the manager to recall Amarnath, who had been ordered to tender an unqualified apology to the captain and manager. When informed of the Board's decision, Vizzy gave his consent saying that he was extremely broad-minded and did not bear any personal malice towards Amarnath.[27]

However, soon after the publication of this report the private secretary of the Nawab of Bhopal issued the following statement to the press:

The attention of the president of the Board of control for Cricket in India has been drawn to a broadcast message from England tonight announcing that news has been received from New Delhi that as a result of the intervention by His Highness the Nawab of Bhopal, Amarnath is returning to England by air to play in the Test match at Manchester. The President wishes to lose no time in informing all concerned that this announcement is wholly unauthorised and premature. No decision has been taken in this connection either by the Board or the President. Amarnath's case is under the consideration of the Board and any decision that may be taken by the proper authorities will, if necessary, be announced in due course to the public. His Highness hopes that no attention will be paid to unauthorised publication of news in this connection.[28]

A couple of days later, on 18 July, the office of the President of the Board of Control issued another statement that declared:

On a private and confidential inquiry by the President, the captain and the manager having agreed to the return of Amarnath on certain conditions, the matter was being considered by the Board. Since then, intimation has been received by the President that his return is undesirable. The question of Amarnath's return has therefore been closed.[29]

On the same day, Vizzy too distributed a statement to the press that stated, 'I am a strict disciplinarian. After agreeing to Amarnath being sent back on certain conditions, deeper considerations changed my mind, and I informed the Board to that effect.'[30]

On the following day E.D.H. Sewell, writing in the *Times of India*, declared:

> I am definitely of the opinion that it will be in the best interests of Indian cricket for Amarnath not to return to England. From information in my possession I take the responsibility of stating the captain does not want him back. It is very doubtful, if he came, whether he would include him in either of the Tests. I have learnt further details, which, in my opinion, debar Amarnath from playing in any eleven anywhere. Sir Vijaya cabled the Nawab of Bhopal stating that the suggested apology by Amarnath was quite inadequate because it deals with only one incident. The captain is quite right. That apart the return now of Amarnath will be unjust to those players here who have played the game, who have tried to get in form in case they are required in the Tests and, above all things, have behaved like gentlemen, giving dignity to Indian cricket and credit to its colours. The Board's authority would have been everlastingly weakened if it gave way. It is quite possible to pardon a wild youngster's offence without sending him back where, so far as I can see, nobody wants him.[31]

Upon being informed that he was not to be sent back, Amarnath, in a bitter outburst against the Board of Control asserted that he thought that his case had not received fair and impartial consideration. He demanded that the Board should conduct an inquiry into the case. In an interview with the cricket correspondent of the *Times of India*, he mentioned that he was willing to make any apology required and had every reason to believe that he would return to England:

> I have no intention of appearing before the board again, as I feel that it will serve no purpose. I am not indispensable to Indian cricket, nobody is, but if I am to come back to international cricket again, I demand that the Board should make an impartial inquiry into my case and obtain an apology from either me or the captain and manager, whichever party is considered guilty. I have continued to play the role of sinner and gone from door to door making apology after apology but to no purpose, and I do not see any reason why the captain and manager should be ashamed to confess their error and publicly express their regret if they are considered to have done wrong. I was made to apologise a dozen times even before the Board had considered

my case, and yet I have not been told by the President that my conduct deserved the treatment given. I therefore consider that I did not merit the punishment.[32]

He stated that till 1.20 p.m. on Saturday 18 July he was under the impression that he was to return to England to join the team. In fact his trunk was sent to Bombay by a special messenger with instructions to send it overland from Marseilles as he was carrying a couple of bats, some flannels and his cricket boots with him. It was only after lunch that he received a message that conveyed to him that he was not to go. When he telephoned the shipping office in Bombay, he was told that his luggage had left by the English mail steamer that afternoon.[33]

He signed off saying:

> As I am completely ignorant of the Board's constitution I cannot say whether all the developments in my case are in keeping with the Board's policy or rules, but I state most emphatically that the entire episode has not been given fair or impartial consideration. Even when I arrived in Bombay I was told that there were wheels within wheels but felt convinced that the President of the Board would have instituted an impartial inquiry and taken advantage of his emergency powers or even be guided by the opinion and decision of a dozen cricket institutions in this country. Now that I have been disgraced publicly I do not make any apology because I know there is no reason for me to apologise. It was only with the object of doing my best for the team that I was anxious to go back signing any form of apology, which would assist me to that end. I was repentant to this extent that my expressions of disgust and annoyance should have been magnified and judged as they have been. Let the Board publish the Manager's report and my statement if they feel that I have been guilty.[34]

Even the Beaumont Committee appointed to deliberate on the controversy found Amarnath guilty and supported Vizzy's and Brittain Jones' action in sending him back on grounds of indiscipline and misbehaviour. To strengthen Vizzy's position, the Committee also declared that prior to the commencement of the tour, Amarnath had sent Vizzy a telegram asking for a loan of Rs. 6,000, which he received, and this was proof that the captain had no malice against him. Amarnath denied these allegations and insisted that a third party, if at all, had sent the telegram. He went on to allege that Vizzy had introduced the subject of the telegram to help explain the unfair disciplinary action taken in England.[35]

Though Amarnath did not get justice in 1936, he did get it later when he served as team captain, and later as chairman of the selection committee.[36] His ultimate reward came when *Wisden* nominated him as one of India's 16 cricketers of the century.[37] Vizzy and Brittain Jones, on the other hand, remain villains, who, using their position of authority, tried wrongly to harm one of the country's best cricketers. One must mention here that harming the nation's leading cricketers was not unheard of in pre-Partition India. Nayudu, perhaps an even bigger star than Amarnath, was treated in a similar manner a year later in 1937, a controversy to which we turn in the next chapter.

5

Nayudu Scorned

Only noble souls can rejoice at the success of others. The attitude of cricketers who were antagonistic to Nayudu has its roots in jealousy, conceit, greed and indiscipline.

D.B. Deodhar on the ill treatment meted out to C.K. Nayudu.[1]

C.K. Nayudu is India's greatest cricketer. Whether it was bowling, batting, fielding, captaincy, physical fitness, positive approach to the game, there will never be Nayudu's equal among Indians. He could play all bowling, more particularly the greatest fast bowler I have played, Mohammed Nissar. His many innings on the Bombay Gymkhana ground where the bowler has as much chance of getting the batsman out as the batsman of making a big score, will forever be remembered. The greater the crisis, the greater was Nayudu and I have never seen him being affected by nerves. It was a pity that during his time there were not many Test matches, otherwise his record in Test cricket would be second to none amongst our cricketers. Judge him by statistics and he was only moderately successful. Judge him by performances when the going was tough and he was our greatest cricketer. There has never been a greater entertainer in a cricket ground, and in my time the name of Nayudu was good enough to draw people from their offices and from their businesses to the Bombay Gymkhana to see him play. I have yet to see an Indian cricketer who inspired greater confidence and remained a dominant personality on the field as long as he played the game. Nayudu's name will be cherished and remembered as long as cricket is played in this country.[2]

Vijay Merchant on C.K. Nayudu.

Imagine the same Vijay Merchant plotting against Nayudu hand in hand with Vizzy. Improbable yes, but true. It happened when Lord Tennyson's Englishmen visited India for an unofficial Test series in November–December 1937. C.K. Nayudu, by far the greatest cricketer

of pre-independence India, was left out of the side through machinations
of power play and corruption.

In an age when the princes controlled Indian cricket, Nayudu, a
commoner, had the audacity to challenge their superiority, and paid the
price for it. In 1932, when India played their first ever Test at Lords,
the Maharaja of Porbander had been forced to step down from the
captaincy in favour of Nayudu. Wisden described his batsmanship in the
following words:

> Tall and well proportioned, Nayudu is eminently fitted by nature to be a good
> cricketer and his doings for the Indian team fully bore out the accounts of
> him that had come to us by reason of his excellent performances in his own
> land. Possessed of supple and powerful wrists and a very good eye, he hit
> that ball tremendously hard but, unlike the modern Australian batsman, he
> lifted it a fair amount. He was also a very fine fielder and showed himself
> admirably suited for the duties of leadership in what were, after all, rather
> difficult circumstances.[3]

The Indian team returned home from this tour having left a favourable
impression in the United Kingdom. Nayudu, commenting on the tour in
the *Bombay Chronicle*, declared, 'Everyday, every way, we learnt some
new lesson or other during our tour of England.'[4]

Then, in 1933–34, when Douglas Jardine's MCC toured India, Nayudu
captained the Indians in the three Test matches at Bombay, Calcutta and
Madras. Though this series was a disappointment for Nayudu, he was
a strong contender for the captaincy during the 1936 tour of England,
but he eventually lost 10:4 to Vizzy in the election.[5] This loss, as was
evident in the previous chapter, was plainly the result of intrigue and saw
one of the worst players in the team being appointed captain. With Vizzy
forever keen to humiliate Nayudu, he had even ordered Baqa Jilani to
abuse Nayudu at the breakfast table promising him his maiden Test cap
if he carried out the orders. The charge that Nayudu did not extend a
hand of cooperation to the captain was baseless. Without recording
Nayudu's evidence or even consulting him, the Beaumont Committee
appointed to probe the 1936 debacle asserted, 'Nayudu held himself
aloof from the team and did not offer any support to the captain.'[6] As
Vasant Raiji states, 'Nayudu was not designated vice-captain nor was he
briefed to play the role of advisor to the captain. Surely, Vizzy would
have received Nayudu's whole-hearted co-operation had he approached
him in the right spirit.'[7] However, the worst controversy involving
Nayudu was to occur about a year later.

After a forgettable tour of England, the Indians faced Lord Tennyson's
men at home in November–December 1937. To everyone's surprise

Nayudu was dropped from the team for the first Test (these were unofficial Tests). The reason given was his string of poor performances in the domestic season. That the reason assigned was a cover-up is evident from the following report:

> The 1936 Quadrangular lacked the glamour of the earlier two years because of the absence of two superstars, Nayudu and Nissar. In 1937 one more team, the Rest, was added and the tournament was now called the Pentangulars. The venue of the matches was shifted from the Bombay Gymkhana to the Brabourne Stadium where the wicket always favoured the batsman.... Because of a dispute over the allocation of seats in the new stadium, the Hindus (who were to be captained by Nayudu) withdrew from the tournament.[8]

Thus Nayudu, absent from the premier domestic competition in 1936 and 1937, could not be dropped for reasons of loss of form. What remained unsaid was that the powers that dominated Indian cricket did not want Nayudu in the team for reasons of their own.

Unfortunately for them India fared miserably without Nayudu. With public opinion firmly against them, the selectors, led by Colonel Mistry, were forced to recall Nayudu for the second Test. Little did they know that they would be forced to reverse their decision soon. In fact, the sequence of events that followed his recall can easily rank as one of the most disgraceful episodes in the history of Indian cricket.

After the selectors had picked the team for the second Test, an official letter was sent to Nayudu on behalf of the Board informing him of his inclusion in the All India XI that would meet Tennyson's XI in the second Test at Bombay. After his selection, one of the selectors even remarked that Nayudu was the only cricketer who would have been able to successfully deal with Alf Gover and Paul Gibb, the bowler-wicketkeeper pair that 'had become terrors for our Test team'. And that it would be a lesson for youngsters to watch Nayudu bat against Australia. Nayudu, always keen to don the national colours, accepted the invitation and arrived in Bombay in time for the match.

Commending his sportsman spirit the *Bombay Sentinel* reported, 'A great sport that he is, he came here setting aside all the grievances and forgetting all the slanderous remarks hurled at him by the Beaumont committee.'[9] However, on the morning of 11 December, the day the Bombay Test began, the Indian public woke up to an official announcement in the newspapers about the exclusion of Nayudu from the team. To add insult to injury, Nayudu had not been informed and only learned of the decision from the papers. He was dropped in favour of Mohammed Sayeed, about whose cricketing abilities nothing much is known.

Why did the selectors pick Nayudu in the first place if they were going to drop him eventually? Apparently the letter was a charade, and the selectors had hoped that Nayudu would not accept the invitation to join the team. When he did accept, the 'enemies of Major Nayudu were nonplussed', the *Sentinel* reported with reference to the princes in whose hands the selectors were mere puppets.[10]

These enemies, it was speculated, also included Nayudu's teammates. Rumour had it that when Amar Singh, who had failed miserably with both bat and ball in the first Test got to know of the invitation, he set about pulling strings. His task was easy because he received full support from Vizzy, by then the leading patron of Indian cricket. Accordingly, those who had sent Nayudu the invitation were soon taken to task.

Emboldened by the support from Vizzy, nine players out of the 14 informed the selection committee that they were unwilling to play with Nayudu in the team. Speaking of Nayudu's enmity with his teammates, Vasant Raiji argued:

> Amarsingh was not keen to play under Nayudu. Colah and Amir Elahi became his enemies during the English tours and there was not much love lost between him and Vinoo Mankad. Nayudu was a superstar and it was but natural that some of his teammates resented the public adulation that he received to the exclusion of others who got relegated to the back stage. Bradman too had to suffer the wrath of some of his colleagues for his immense popularity.[11]

Commenting on the same issue J.C. Maitra wrote in the *Bombay Chronicle*:

> It is an open secret that during the England tour of 1932 some of the Indian players threw all barriers of discipline to the winds. Keeping late hours and getting drunk were with them ordinary features of the day. Even when they did not restrain themselves before a Test match, C.K. Nayudu as their captain called them to order and threatened to keep them out of the Test, if they did not behave themselves. He also appealed to them in the name of India's honour. This instead of acting as a restraining influence on them infuriated them still more. It is said there were squabbles and fights thereafter over this and the recalcitrant members pledged themselves to be after Nayudu's blood ever since.[12]

Further, as Raiji affirmed:

> After the first Test against England in 1933–34 Amarsingh stated that he wanted to enjoy cricket, not to win at all costs. He liked to entertain the spectators and give them good value for their money but Nayudu made the

game such a kill-joy pursuit that he just did not feel able to try. Can Nayudu be blamed for taking Test cricket seriously and not in a light hearted manner?[13]

What was surprising was that Vijay Merchant, who was the captain and one of the three selectors, allowed the injustice to pass. Had Merchant so desired he could have dictated to the Selection Committee, which consisted of the Nawab of Pataudi, Colonel Mistry and himself. But all that Merchant cared for was to establish himself as India's star batsman, and for his friend Amar Singh to get some wickets.

Merchant duly came in for plenty of criticism for his part in the affair. The *Sentinel*'s correspondent voiced common sentiment when he declared, 'It is very doubtful if ever he will get back the popularity he once enjoyed.'[14] When Merchant was dismissed cheaply in the Test the *Sentinel* remarked, 'The curse of the 35,000 who had gathered to watch the match seems to have worked…. I have yet to come across a man who was sorry at Merchant getting out early.'[15]

Cricket enthusiasts and the press were firmly behind Nayudu. A number of letters published in the dailies expressed admiration for Nayudu and condemned princely interference in Indian cricket. One of these letters, addressed to Colonel Mistry asked:

> If you were not sure of his inclusion in the team why did you at all call him? Was it to insult the veteran and disregard public opinion? Secondly, we have a strong doubt that it might be a player or group of players who threatened the selection committee that they would stay back if CK was included. If this be the case, leave out those players who have no sportsmanship and spirit of sacrifice….[16]

Nayudu had emerged from the controversy a greater hero than ever before. 'Attempts deliberately to insult and humiliate the Indian Jessop would only hasten the day when those at present in charge of Indian cricket will nowhere be near it,' the *Sentinel* declared.[17] There was also speculation that had Nayudu played in the second Test, which India lost by six wickets, the result would have been the reverse. What was ominous for the Board was that sections of the public felt that they had been hoodwinked. Thousands who had arrived in Bombay just to see Nayudu play, taking advantage of the railway concessions provided for the occasion felt cheated when they heard he was not in the team and felt it was all a ploy by the Board to boost the gate money collections.

From condemning the actions of the Selection Committee and the captain, the fans went on to demand that Nayudu be made captain for the third Test against the Australians to be played at Calcutta. The *Bombay Sentinel* led the charge, 'Let Major Nayudu skipper the team in the third Test and the victory will be ours. This will to some extent go to compensate for the gross injustice done to him.'[18] Expressing a similar view the *Star of India* remarked, 'The public will not take the Nayudu affair lying down. It means more than what it superficially signifies. Nayudu humiliated means India humiliated.'[19]

Though Nayudu was not picked for the rest of the series, his popularity, by the end of the English tour was far greater than that of Merchant who lost the series 3–2 to the second-string English side. In fact, Merchant, to redeem himself, was forced to admit his mistake in public and apologise to Nayudu for the wrong done to him.[20]

Nayudu, who did not play a single Test match after this, returned to captain the Hindus in the Pentangular of 1938 playing one of his best innings in the process. Vasant Raiji, an eyewitness, described the innings thus, 'In 1938, I watched Nayudu's beautiful cameo, an innings of 66, again against Nissar. Nayudu batting against Nissar is the finest spectacle I have ever seen on the cricket field.'[21]

Nayudu was felicitated with a reasonable purse by most cricket associations of the country on the occasion of his 25th year in first-class cricket in 1941–42. He was chief guest at various functions on numerous occasions in the 1940s, a rare distinction for cricketers then.[22] The esteem in which he was held becomes clear from the following description:

In 1944–45 when Nayudu was fifty, his Golden Jubilee was celebrated with great éclat both in Bombay and Calcutta. In his honour a match between CK Nayudu's XI and the C.C.I was staged in Bombay at the Brabourne Stadium. A purse was presented to him by the cricket loving public of Bombay on the occasion. In 1955, in recognition of Nayudu's services to Indian cricket, the President of India conferred on him the award of Padma Bhushan. In 1973–74 the Board of Control for Cricket in India named a tournament after him. The tournament is conducted on the lines of the Ranji Trophy for those under 22. The trophy was donated by the Bombay Cricket Association from the funds collected to perpetuate the memory of the great cricketer. Nagpur, Nayudu's birthplace honoured him by unveiling his bust in the square near the Vidarbha Cricket Association grounds and naming a street after him. Indore, the city to which he later migrated to serve Holkar and in which he lived for the rest of his life, erected a life size statue of their illustrious citizen at the entrance to the Nehru Stadium. The C.C.I named their banquet hall after him.[23]

Nayudu was also one of the first Indian cricketers to endorse commercial brands. One of the earliest promotions for the Tea Market Expansion Board went thus:

Major C.K. Nayudu, India's greatest cricketer says, 'I have always found a good cup of tea a great refresher during a game of cricket, hockey, soccer, tennis or any other game. It is a great stimulant of the mild and harmless kind. I strongly advocate this beverage to those partake in any strenuous game. Tea is the only drink I love. I cannot do without my tea in the morning and evening.'[24]

C.K. Nayudu continued playing first-class cricket into his sixties,[25] captaining Holkar to four Ranji Trophy victories in the 1940s and 1950s, and is today universally acknowledged as one of the greatest Indian cricketers that ever lived.

6

Tour de Farce

After the tragic example of Rajputana, the cricket authorities in India must see to it that no further unofficial tour is allowed to take place without the participants realizing that they will forfeit all rights of playing first class cricket in India. The time has come to speak out candidly about this ill fated expedition which Mr. W.D. Begg led from Ajmer and which has reached total collapse with half the programme unfulfilled. Nearly every circumstance attending the tour has been deplorable. There is scarcely a redeeming feature anywhere.[1]

This tragic controversy dates back to 1934 when W.D. Begg of the Rajputana Cricket Club asked permission from the Board to take a team of young cricketers on a tour of England.[2] Such unofficial tours had been a long-established tradition in Indian cricket and the just intentions of Begg were lauded in many quarters. Mr. S.C. Roy of Calcutta even went on to promise Begg Rs. 10,000 to meet some of the costs of the tour.[3]

When all seemed set, A.S. De Mello, the secretary of the Board, announced that the Board did not approve of private tours, either at home or abroad. Declaring that they were burdens on the Board's exchequer, De Mello was firm in asserting that the Board would do everything possible to check Begg from going ahead with the proposed tour.[4] De Mello's position was strengthened by the publication of media reports condoning the tour:

It is a pity that a cricket tour to England has been organized which has not the blessing of the Indian Cricket Board of Control. Unofficial tours have been strongly deprecated by the Imperial Cricket Conference. The programme arranged for the Indians in England should afford the younger members of the side useful experience and perhaps assist in developing their cricketing talent, even though the team may not meet a first class side. Moreover an unofficial tour to England during the year when an Australian team is touring the country appears to be unwise.[5]

However, when in the very next year the Maharaja of Patiala wanted to bring out a team of Australian cricketers under Jack Ryder to India, De Mello promptly altered this decision. The Australian trip went ahead undisturbed in October–November 1935 and was key to Patiala re-establishing himself as the key figure in Indian cricket. Thereafter the Board also permitted the Cricket Club of India to arrange for Lord Tennyson's Englishmen to visit India in November–December 1937. Both these visits, which did not have official status, resulted in heavy financial losses for the Board. The refusal to sanction the proposed Rajputana tour cost Begg Rs. 5,000, a heavy sum by contemporary standards.[6]

The decision to disallow the tour had made the Board unpopular and public opinion was firmly aligned against it. Realising that the ordinary cricket fan was against the Board's decision, De Mello relented, allowing Begg to go ahead with the tour in May–June 1938. Having associated itself with the tour, it was now the Board's duty to ensure that the tour went ahead smoothly. However, the Board did nothing to guarantee its success and the trip turned out to be the most disgraceful tour ever undertaken. All the same, when the Rajputana team first arrived in England,

> everybody was willing to give it a fair chance. The official souvenir devoted many pages to the five or six years spadework done by Begg and his helpers, the formidable lists of supporters and their messages of goodwill and the spectacular portraits of patrons. Everybody was impressed at this triumph of achievement in the face of obstacles and opposition. Here indeed was a story well calculated to arouse the Englishman's spirit of fair play.[7]

However, there was much that was wrong with the team to begin with. A team, which claimed to consist of young players, had in its ranks veterans like the Nawab of Pataudi, Ramji and Botawala. Given Pataudi's influence and social status, the Board could hardly raise a voice against this anomaly. Further, after the horrible experience of Vizzy's team in the UK, the Beaumont Committee, appointed to investigate the debacle, had stated that no touring party should consist of more than 16 players. The Rajputana team included in its ranks 20 players to play 22 games, a variance the Board allowed to pass. Later, the inclusion of an unusually high number of players resulted in tremendous internal discord within the team. With each player having paid Rs. 500 towards the expense of the tour, it was natural that most would want more than a handful of games to demonstrate their talent.[8] Eventually, players like Asad Wahab and G. Qureshi got three games each while Sultan Abbas got a solitary one.[9] The decision to take 22 players was severely condemned by the media:

> To take twenty-two players, however, means that a complete team will be cooling their heels in the pavilion. This is liable to breed discontent and cause friction. Some of the players are long past their best and could have made way for younger cricketers. It is doubtful if the strength of the side is equal to that of a good class club side in England.[10]

Expressing similar sentiments another report declared:

> A glance at the list betrayed genuine reasons for skepticism. Here were 20 players for 22 matches involving 33 days actual cricket. This meant that even with the fairest division no individual could rightly expect more than 11 games or 20 days of cricket. Would they be self sacrificing enough? Would the selection of the elevens be free from discrimination?[11]

It was also stated that it was quite evidently not a Rajputana team. Only eight of the 20 players originated from Ajmer, Jaipur and other adjoining territories. Sind had a contingent of five; Bengal had sent two while others came from the United Provinces, Ahmedabad, Kathiawar and Delhi.[12]

This put the Board in an embarrassing position, summed up adequately by J.C. Maitra in the *Bombay Chronicle*.

> Unfortunately the Board of Control would never learn a lesson from past experience. If they had put their foot down when they saw these breaches of their directions the world would not have seen the repetition of those and perhaps much worse scenes which marred Vizzy's tour. There have been squabbles and wranglings among some of the players for places in the team before every match was to be played.[13]

The tour had started well with the Rajputana side winning the first two games. Kartik Bose of Bengal gave a very good account of his batting prowess scoring an unbeaten 131 in the second match of the tour against the Grasshoppers Cricket Club at the Oval.[14] Ironically, everything started to go wrong for the touring side before the match against the Indian Gymkhana. When the Gymkhana decided not to pay for the lunch and tea of the visiting side, which the secretary of the Gymkhana denied later, the Rajputana team, feeling insulted, refused to take the field. It was only after a protracted telephone conversation between Jehangir Khan, the Gymkhana captain, and W.D. Begg, that the problem was sorted out and the match, due to have started at 10 in the morning, finally got underway at 2.20 in the afternoon. This unfortunate incident was thus reported by the *Times of India*:

> Rajputana were due to play their first encounter with the Indian Gymkhana on May 11 and something queer went wrong to convert this full day fixture into a less than half day farce. The trouble originated out of a decision of the Gymkhana committee not to depart from its traditional policy of expecting visiting teams to pay for their own luncheons and tea, as is the general common practice in ordinary club cricket in London. This decision was conveyed in unfortunately worded terms to the Rajputana manager without the Gymkhana players having a chance to arrange among themselves to act as hosts. Rajputana promptly felt insulted and whereas the Gymkhana team turned up in full strength at Osterley, Rajputana sulked all morning in their hotel. Protracted telephone conversations ensued and suddenly Mr. Begg gave way and two Gymkhana members went to fetch the visitors even paying their fares to the ground—a most improper arrangement for the Rajputana side to have insisted upon and accepted.[15]

In fact many within the Rajputana team had opposed the decision arguing that they were giving a very poor account of themselves by refusing to field a team.[16] Even when the match started, the team gave a poor account of themselves on the field:

> Anyhow Rajputana arrived at Osterley where lunch awaited them. They refused to consume it even though they won the toss and elected to bat. The innings started at 2.20 p.m. and Rajputana were all out for a paltry 118 with a belated lunch interrupting play at 3.30 p.m. The Gymkhana reply was interrupted by a deferred tea at 6 p.m. and on the stroke of 7 p.m. Rajputana insisted on stumps being drawn with the Gymkhana requiring seven runs for victory with nine wickets in hand. What should have been a most enjoyable match between two sides of brother Indians thus became converted into a miserably unsporting affair.[17]

When the Board was informed of the incident they pretended to ignore it stating that they had nothing to do with the tour.

From 24 May onwards began the really unhappy chapter in this tragic tour. By then differences had begun to arise within the team on questions of captaincy and selection of elevens for various matches. Things got worse in early June, evinced from a report in the *Daily Express* that the Rajputana team was in danger of getting stranded in London because they had no money to pay their hotel bills. That their assertion was true was soon evident when the team cancelled fixtures against West and East Norfolk for want of funds but played against Cambridge who paid them

£150 for the match. Again the Board expressed indifference about what was happening provoking serious criticism in the media.[18] J.C. Maitra asserted in the *Bombay Chronicle* that:

> It may be argued by the supporters of the Board of Control that the latter could not be held responsible for the acts of the Rajputana team. My answer to this is that it is the clear duty of the controlling body to check and prevent actions by their constituent and subordinate parts.[19]

With the Board staying indifferent, it wasn't a surprise that the tour had to be called off midway. Commenting on the calling off, the special correspondent of the *Times of India* ranted:

> Within three days of these lines being written the members of the team are due to embark on the Anchor liner ELYSIA—unless a last minute miracle occurs. Even on the question of passage there is still uncertainty. As matters have turned out, it is indeed better that the team should go back rather than remain in England whereas the whole enterprise has thoroughly discredited the name of Indian cricket. This may sound severe condemnation. It is intended to convey that impression. The team should never have come for it has all along contained within itself and within its system of organization the germs of discord, failure and disintegration.[20]

The calling off was decided upon all of a sudden, evident from a report published in the *Times of India*:

> From information available here it is learned that the Rajputana Cricket XI, at present playing a series of matches in England have cancelled their remaining fixtures and are expected to arrive in India by July. It is understood that owing to financial troubles the team had to cut short all their engagements in England.[21]

Eventually the team left the British shores on 2 July amidst utter confusion:

> Only a handful of sympathisers witnessed the departure of the Rajputana team when they entrained on Saturday, 2 July, at Euston by the 11.50 a.m. Express to Liverpool where at 4.00 p.m. they embarked on the S.S. Elysia, which sailed an hour later for India. There might have been a better sending off but so swift and sudden had been the course of events in the last few days that few members of the Indian community in London were fully aware of what was happening. Unhappy days they were for the team. Days full of doubt, alarm and anxiety, which at times developed into utter consternation.[22]

Another report published on 4 July asserted, 'The Rajputana Cricket Club team, which was touring England have left for India. A recent

London message stated that owing to a breakdown in their financial arrangements they had been compelled to cancel their remaining fixtures.'[23]

When it became known that the team was on its way back from
England headlines like 'Rajputana tour discredits Indian cricket'[24] and
'Unhappy return of the Rajputana cricket team from England'[25] brought
much disgrace to the Board. Summing up the tour, the *Times of India*
affirmed:

> There were several amazing anomalies during the tour. The tour ended in
> a financial fiasco and a complete breakdown of the team spirit and it is
> difficult to decide whether it benefited any individual player. Certainly no
> good bowler was unearthed. Apart from the financial muddle the organizers'
> initial error consisted in having brought a team much too big and much too
> varied in quality for a second rate programme. That 'come one and come
> all' policy was in itself bound to create difficulties. The participants appear
> to have stepped blindly into a venture whose scope they failed to realize.[26]

Following the cancellation of the tour, the *Bombay Chronicle* mounted
a serious attack on the Board:

> We have no doubt every lover of cricket in India will feel exceedingly ashamed
> at the abrupt termination of the England tour of the Rajputana Cricket Team.
> After the regrettable spectacle presented by Vizzy's team in 1936 we had
> hoped that such episodes would be a thing of the past and the history of the
> last tour would soon be thrown into the limbo of oblivion. But we had
> counted without our ruling body of cricket. If they do not do wrong things
> at the wrong moment and in this wrong manner they would not be what they
> are! In writing so bitterly against the Board of Control for Cricket in India
> we are not exaggerating the state of public feelings in the least. They have
> hopelessly betrayed the cause for which they are supposed to stand.[27]

It was also stated that it was no good suggesting that private tours
would not be allowed in future:

> Saying no to private tours is an absurd proposition. We do not see any reason
> why a private tour should not be permitted if satisfactory guarantees on all
> points are forthcoming from its promoters. It is not possible for the Board
> of Control to promote a vast number of foreign tours themselves. At the same
> time it is recognized on all hands that foreign tours have a great educative
> value and for a comparatively backward country like India it is absolutely
> necessary.[28]

The criticisms against the Board hardly proved effective as the Board
was once again involved in a major controversy in a couple of years—
this time over the banning of the Bombay Pentangular tournament.

7

The Pentangular Panned

Ever since the early 1930s, the Bombay Pentangular, the foremost tournament in pre-Partition India, had been a favourite whipping horse in the Indian cricket world, the target of frenzied rhetoric of contemporaries and staid denunciation of later commentators.

The Bombay Pentangular, controlled by the communal Gymkhanas,[1] had its inception in the Presidency matches of the 1890s.[2] In course of time, the Pentangular tournament came into existence, with the inclusion of the Hindus in 1907, the Muslims in 1912 and the 'Rest' comprising mainly Christians and Anglo-Indians in 1937. Despite considerable opposition, the tournament continued till January 1946, when it was finally abolished.[3]

The communal nature of the Pentangular, its detractors argued, was inimical to the spirit of the emerging secular nation. Echoing these sentiments, the *Bombay Chronicle* of 27 November 1935 declared, 'Communal tournaments were, perhaps, necessary at a certain stage in the history of Indian cricket. Scarcely conducive to the growth of healthy nationalism, it is time they were given a decent burial.'[4]

Its sports editor, J.C. Maitra, consistently wrote in support of the Ranji Trophy and against the continuation of the Pentangular.[5] Another renowned sports journalist, J.M. Ganguly expressed similar views in his article: 'Quadrangular Cricket—A Plea for its Abolition' published in *Indian Cricket* (1938), the mouthpiece of the Cricket Club of India:

When the Quadrangular matches were conceived and started times were different; the sports atmosphere was clear and unclouded by communal and sectarian feelings.... Those happy days are now gone, thanks to those self seeking leaders who want to gain their ends by raking up communal fanaticism, and who would not rest on their oars after doing all the mischief they could in the political sphere but would go out in search of new fields and pastures green. Even the sacred field of sport they would not leave unmolested.[6]

Echoing similar sentiments Berry Sarbadhikary argued:

> Communal cricket must go by the board and be buried—five fathoms deep. That is as things stand to day. There might not have been, at the outset, anything 'communal' about communal cricket in the accepted sense of the word as Anthony S. De. Mello submitted when the controversy had been raging fiercely and fully a few years ago. There may not be anything communal about it even today so far as the players and spectators are concerned as has been laboriously claimed with the aid of a whole heap of evidence. But the fact remains that once the controversy gathered the fierceness and the momentum it did, once communal cricket was dissected and decried or patched up and praised by politicians or cricketers, by the press and the public in the manner it was done, communal cricket became communal straightaway. Only communal cricket is basically wrong and although synonymous with the cream of Indian cricket once, it has now outlived its usefulness, to say nothing of its being not indispensable to Indian cricket any more.[7]

The anti-Pentangular controversy intensified with Gandhi's pronouncement against the tournament in December 1940. On being met by a select delegation of the Hindu Gymkhana at Wardha, the Mahatma had remarked:

> Numerous enquiries have been made as to my opinion on the proposed Pentangular cricket match in Bombay advertised to be played on the 14th. I have just been made aware of the movement to stop the match. I understand this as a mark of grief over the arrests and imprisonments of the satyagrahis, more especially the recent arrest of leaders.[8]

He went on to add:

> I would discountenance such amusements at a time when the whole of the thinking world should be in mourning over a war that is threatening the stable life of Europe and its civilisation and which bids to overwhelm Asia.... And holding this view I naturally welcome the movement for stopping the forthcoming match from the narrow standpoint I have mentioned above.[9]

It was after this statement, prompted by nationalist sentiments that he went on to condemn the communal nature of the tournament.

Gandhi's stand in this matter seems to lack consistency when we compare it with his avowed ideal of keeping sport away from political interference. His view that amusements should be stopped at a critical juncture (in this case during the Second World War) reflects a clear case of 'politicisation of sport' by the Mahatma himself. Further, the reason for abolition advanced by the Mahatma is rooted in anti-imperial rhetoric, a sentiment made clear by K.M. Munshi at a Prohibition Guards Party before Gandhi's assertion. Referring to the approaching carnival he had stated:

> When India is denied the right of being a comrade of Britain in war, when 1500 elected representatives of your country have decided to prefer to be locked up in British jails, I ask, 'Will you be able to enjoy the Pentangular? Will not the cricket carnival be exploited by those who are against your country by telling the world that whatever your elected representatives may do the people are so happy and reconciled to their unfortunate lot that they have time to go and enjoy cricket matches?'[10]

Resonating Gandhian overtones of passive resistance, this assertion clearly seeks to use the Pentangular as a tool of non-violent resistance against the unjust policies of the colonial state.

Within a couple of weeks of Gandhi's pronouncement, the Maharajkumar of Vizianagram declared, 'Mahatma Gandhi has expressed unequivocally on communal cricket. He gave it as his considered opinion that communalism carried into the domain of sport is no happy augury for human growth. It is high time that we gave Pentangular cricket the burial it always deserved.'[11] He was supported by the Jam of Nawanagar and the Maharaja of Patiala, who went on to assert that no Nawanagar or Patiala player would be available for any match conducted on communal lines. Cricketers employed by these princes, it was expected, would not have the audacity to defy their orders. Following them, Dr. Subbaraon, the President of the Board, asserted in the *Bombay Chronicle* of 10 December 1940:

> I did not want to say anything about the Pentangular though the matter was referred to me as I felt that it might be said that I took this opportunity to achieve what I have in mind, but now that Mahatmaji has spoken, I feel free to say that the authorities will be doing the right thing if they abandon communal cricket.

Despite these pronouncements against the competition, there were no signs of declining interest in the Pentangular matches. The very next day after Gandhi issued his statement, the *Times of India* reported:

> With Bombay's great annual cricket festival only a few days ahead the Pentangular fever is at its height, a height that has rarely been attained before. Large crowds watched all the three trial matches played over the weekend.... Although rumours had been set afoot that there would be a serious attempt

made by a large procession of students to compel the authorities to abandon the trial more than 500 enthusiasts gathered on Saturday afternoon for the start, and the number was almost doubled the next day.[12]

When a resolution was tabled at the Hindu Gymkhana calling for a withdrawal from the tournament in 1940, it had the support of only 70 out of a total of 900 members of the Gymkhana. Though this resolution was eventually passed by a small margin of 37 votes (280:243), particularly as a mark of regard for Gandhi's pronouncement against the tournament, it generated serious ill feeling among the members themselves.[13] A prominent member of the Gymkhana, who had supported the resolution, stated later that the managing committee of the Gymkhana had been unwise in deciding to seek Gandhi's opinion on the subject.[14] Further, Gandhi's stand had provoked considerable opposition from the small Hindu cricket clubs of Bombay. Many of these clubs, which barely managed to eke out an existence on the profits accruing from the Pentangular, (profits often running into a lakh) had already invested their meagre capital in securing seats at the Brabourne stadium, the venue for the tournament. In the event of the withdrawal of the Hindus from the competition, interest was expected to wane to such an extent as to make the sale of tickets impossible, and would bring in its wake ruin for these clubs. This, it was argued, would be unfair in view of the wholehearted support accorded by the Hindus and Hindu clubs, both in Bombay and in the mofussil, to the Hindu Gymkhana in times of crisis. These clubs emphasised that the Hindu Gymkhana should not overlook the fact that it was a Hindu representative XI that was expected to participate in the Pentangular, and not a Hindu Gymkhana team. Accordingly, it was regarded inconceivable that any drastic action could be implemented on the decision of the 900-odd members of the Hindu Gymkhana alone. A decision that was expected to affect thousands of Hindus, it was agreed, was expected to take into account their interests and opinion.[15] This body of opinion, expressing surprise at the decision to consult Gandhi, went on to state:

> We respect Mr. Gandhi's opinion in politics as being that of a great statesman and patriot, but when he offers it in connection with cricket and the Pentangular, about which he himself pleads ignorance, we feel he has no local standing.[16]

Expressing dissatisfaction over the actions of the Hindu Gymkhana in a meeting convened by the Bombay Hindu cricket clubs, they adopted a series of resolutions supporting the Pentangular.[17] The tenor of these resolutions shows that the primary factor behind their support to the

Pentangular was its commercial potential, a fact ubiquitously overlooked in existing literature on the subject:

> This meeting of the Bombay Hindu Cricket Clubs is of the opinion that the Hindus should take part in the ensuing Pentangular tournament, as the non-participation of the Hindus in this year's tournament will lead to serious financial loss to the Hindu cricket clubs in particular and the Hindu public in general.
>
> In the event of the P.J. Hindu Gymkhana deciding not to participate in this year's Pentangular, this meeting requests the Bombay Cricket Association to reconsider the minimum charges fixed for the sale of tickets, and further requests the Gymkhana to fix its rates in consultation with the representatives of this Union.[18]

Even the players strongly supported the continuation of the tournament. Having realised that a victory in the tournament would give them considerable socio-economic prosperity, stalwarts like Wazir Ali, Mushtaq Ali and C.K. Nayudu rooted for the continuation of the tournament.

In November 1940, Wazir Ali, the captain of the Muslim team, issued a press statement claiming that 'the tournament is not in the least anti-national and will and must go on in the interests of Indian cricket'.[19] In the very next year in November 1941, C.K. Nayudu declared, 'There is no valid reason why the Pentangular tournament in Bombay should be stopped. On the contrary it is absolutely essential that it should be run in its present form if we do not want to see the funeral of Indian cricket.'[20] He concluded saying:

> the Pentangular provides a fortnight of first class cricket and is in my opinion the greatest cricket tournament in the world. It would indeed be a pity and the certain death of Indian cricket if the Pentangular were abolished at the present time when Indian players have so little opportunity of playing first class cricket.'[21]

The continuing popularity of the Pentangular draws our attention to a different facet of the anti-Pentangular controversy. Sifting through the layers of politically correct rhetoric one comes upon astounding evidence that suggests that far from being propelled by the declared honourable intentions, the anti-Pentangular agitation, led by the native aristocracy and the leaders of the Board of Control, was also motivated by commercial intentions and politics.

It is recorded that in 1924, when the Muslims won the Pentangular tournament, the Hindus had joined them in their victory celebrations. This was despite the strained relations between the two communities after the failure of the joint Non-Cooperation/Khilafat agitation. In an atmosphere of growing communal contrariety in the country, Mohammed Ali Jinnah had hailed the brotherly feeling between the two communities in view on the sporting field of the Pentangular (then the Quadrangular) in 1924.[22] Even after the final of the 1944 tournament, which the Muslims won with less than five minutes of the match remaining, communalism was nowhere in evidence. Everyone, including the Hindus, cheered the Muslim team at the end of the match. This is borne out by the following eyewitness account of the 1944 Pentangular by Vasant Raiji:

> Unprecedented scenes of jubilation followed. Ibrahim, the hero and architect of the Muslim victory (he had carried his bat for 137) was chaired by the supporters and carried shoulder high all the way to the pavilion. Never before had the Brabourne stadium witnessed a match so thrilling and exciting as this. Communalism was nowhere in evidence and everyone, including the Hindus, cheered the Muslim team at the end of the match. Merchant, the Hindu captain, went to the Muslim dressing room and hugged Mushtaq Ali warmly with the words, 'Well played Muslims, you deserved to win. It would have been a sad day for cricket if you had lost.'[23]

Suspicions regarding the noble motives of the patrician lobby who opposed the Pentangular acquire potency because the commercially successful Bombay Pentangular was singled out by them and attacked while similar 'communal' tournaments continued to be played in Sind, the Central Provinces and Berar.[24] Significantly, it was around this time that the Congress government in Bombay converted swimming baths in the city into communal ones, with separate bathing times for Hindus, Muslims and Parsees.[25] The absence of protest against this action of the Congress government makes it evident that the criticism of the Pentangular by the protesters, though couched in the politically correct idiom of secularism, was, in fact, the result of other considerations. Echoing these sentiments Sir Homi Mody, presiding over the 10th Annual General Meeting of the Cricket Club of India in 1944, strongly criticised the opposing lobby. He asserted:

> We have a set of critics in Bombay who have no eyes or ears for the many communal institutions, which flourish in our midst and the many communal fixtures that are staged throughout the country. The gaze of these people is fixed upon the Pentangular and they return again and again to attack it.[26]

Another aspect of the controversy was the dispute over the radio commentary of the Pentangular which amply demonstrated the commercial potential of the tournament. The radio commentary of the Pentangular was banned, and replaced with a commentary of the less popular Ranji

Trophy. This ban had a vital commercial significance, evident from the concern expressed by the All India Radio merchants:

> The trade views this development with deepest concern. The trade is in the best position to judge the great interest taken all over India in these running commentaries of Bombay's famous cricket festival and views with apprehension a move that gravely affects its business.[27]

Consequently, they urged a fresh review of the entire situation stating, 'There is still ample time to arrange for the famous broadcasts and thus make available to the public of India the commentaries that are the most looked forward to radio events of the year by every class, community or creed.'[28] The opposition to the Pentangular reached a climax when the United Provinces Cricket Association passed the following resolution in 1942:

> It is felt on all hands that the time has come when concerted action should be taken to rid the country of the canker of communal cricket as it tends to retard unity and good fellowship in the country. Is it not deplorable for Hindus to play against their Muslim brethren and vice versa? The cream of Indian cricketers participate in the Pentangular and these players belong to the various provinces which are affiliated to the Board of Control as the Governing body. The Board, as constituted with these affiliating units, should come to a decision by which a player who participates in communal cricket shall not, for the rest of his cricketing career, be eligible to play for his own province or his country in any official match that may be staged or any tournament that is run under the auspices of the Provincial Association concerned or the Board.[29]

This resolution marked the beginning of a concerted campaign against the Pentangular, which reached its head when the government threatened to intervene if the Pentangular committee continued with the tournament. The Board, which had favourable relations with the government, ensured that its protests against the Pentangular had official sanction, and this was significant in the eventual closure of the competition in 1946. Such protests, however, had very little impact on the popularity of the Pentangular tournament. A *Times of India* report affirms this:

> There appears to be no doubt as to the popularity of this season's cricket festival. Youthful picketers resumed their efforts to dissuade enthusiasts from entering the Brabourne stadium, but they were good humouredly ignored and an even bigger crowd than on the previous morning greeted the rival teams on the commencement of play, a crowd steadily increasing until it was somewhat in the vicinity of the twenty thousand mark during the afternoon.[30]

Unable to contend with the growing popularity of the Pentangular, the Board had been forced to call an Extra-Ordinary General Meeting in January 1942 to obtain the support of cricket associations countrywide for banning the Pentangular. At the general meeting the following resolution was tabled:

> The Board considers that time has come when concerted action should be taken to rid the country of the canker of communal cricket as it tends to retard unity of good fellowship in the country, and as the first step in that direction it views with strong disfavour any tournament or match being played on communal lines and calls upon its affiliated associations to co-operate in this respect and take all necessary steps to stop such matches and tournaments.[31]

This resolution understandably provoked serious opposition from the representative of the Bombay Cricket Association. Mr. H.N. Contractor, representing Bombay, retorted that the Bombay Pentangular organised by the communal Gymkhanas under the aegis of the Bombay Cricket Association was an autonomous tournament and the Board had no power to interfere with its internal management. He asserted that the guiding principles of the Board precluded it from tampering with the conduct of any tournament run independently, especially, one, which had been in existence since long before the Board had been formed. He pointed out that the main tenet of the Board's resolution was political, being directed exclusively against the commercially successful Bombay Pentangular.[32]

Following the above response, Pankaj Gupta of the Bengal Gymkhana, representing the interests of the Board, moved the following amendment:

> The Board of Control for Cricket in India, on a matter of principle and in the larger interests of the country deplores any cricket festival or tournament and all matches run on lines, which may, or are likely to, lead to unhealthy communal rivalry. The Board resolves to appoint a sub-committee to formulate schemes for an alternate tournament for its consideration, and adoption if necessary.[33]

At this Mr. Contractor again expressed doubt as to whether the Board had the authority to interfere with the activities of a provincial association, in whatever capacity it may be. He went on to state that if the Board forcibly enforced the resolution, it would lead to a parting of ways between the Board and the Bombay Cricket Association.[34] This assertion clearly shows the confidence of the Bombay Cricket Association, which was in no way dependent on the Board for its well being. Contradicting the main tenets of the resolution that communal cricket generated communal antagonism, Contractor narrated his experience of the 1936 Quadrangular. This tournament was played at a time when Bombay was experiencing bitter communal riots. Despite such strife in the city, the Pentangular (then Quadrangular) did not cause a single unpleasant incident. On the contrary, the tournament helped to cement amity between the members of the two communities and had 'ameliorated the estranged feelings by smoothing the hot atmosphere and had actually ended the serious riots'.[35]

In the face of opposition, Dr. Subbaraon, the President of the Board, announced his decision to resign if the resolution was not passed. He also justified the actions of the princes, who, he felt, had had the nation's interests in mind when they had banned players from taking part in the communal Pentangular.[36]

With a rift between the Board and the Bombay Cricket Association looming large, Pankaj Gupta appealed to the Bombay Cricket Association not to oppose the Board. The Board's decision, whether good or bad, was to be obeyed by all regional associations in the country. Despite his plea, the representatives of the Bombay Cricket Association were relentless, and emphatic that the Board was doing a grave wrong. Failing to impose their decision on the Bombay Cricket Association, the Board finally decided to withdraw the resolution and appoint a select committee to deliberate on the question of communal cricket.[37]

This committee after much deliberation on the issue argued in the next meeting of the Board on 15 March 1942 that the controlling body was empowered to take any step deemed necessary to discontinue the holding of any tournament by any member association within its jurisdiction. It asked the member associations responsible for the management of communal tournaments to put an immediate stop to them, failing which the Board would be forced to intervene. At the same time, however, fearing that the Bombay Cricket Association might decide to break away from the control of the Board, the sub-committee was forced to make concessions, contradicting its own stand in the process:

> The structure of Bombay and Sind cricket being on communal lines, this sub-committee further considers that relaxation of the principle set forth above may be made in case of Bombay, Sind or any other association in order to follow the principle that there should be no interference normally in the internal administration of any member association, provided the tournament concerned is confined to players in the area of the association concerned on the lines of the rules of the Sind Pentangular.[38]

Despite such concessions, Contractor expressed dissent, arguing that the more the Board tried to legislate on matters beyond its jurisdiction and interfere in the internal affairs of a provincial body, the more difficult it would become for the Board to retain its position. The Bombay Cricket Association, he asserted, had never intervened in the affairs of the communal Gymkhanas that controlled the running of the Pentangular.[39]

Representing Sind, Mr. Sohrab Mehta echoed similar sentiments arguing that if the Board had no objection to communal cricket being played by players of a certain area, there was no reason why the Bombay Pentangular tournament should be subjected to criticism.[40]

The conflict between the Board and the Bombay Cricket Association did not abate, eventually resulting in the withdrawal of Bombay from the National Championships in November 1942. Bombay's refusal to participate provoked a hostile reaction in most quarters of the country because most of the other associations, less favourably financially endowed than Bombay, had consented to participate in the championships. The chief reason behind Bombay's refusal to participate as reported by the *Times of India* was fear of serious financial loss.[41] This decision had the support of the players. Vijay Merchant, captain of the Bombay team, was the chief advocate behind the move to stay away from the national championships, a decision that may have resulted in his suspension by the Board. 'Merchant laid great stress on the danger of wrecking and it was even put to the managing committee that players themselves were against the idea of Bombay's participation.'[42]

It is possible to read into this decision an attempt by the players to take on the might of the Board. Aggrieved at the Board's attempts to thwart the Pentangular, the players had consciously decided to boycott the national championships organised by it. Their attempts were largely successful, as the following statement by K.S. Ranga Rao, the Honorary Secretary of the Board reveals:

> The recommendations of the Bombay Cricket Association to abandon the Ranji Trophy for this year has been circulated to all associations for their views and a majority of them have expressed themselves in favour of holding the all India championships as usual.
>
> It is needless for the Board to stress how important the Ranji Trophy is for the furtherance of cricket in India, in view of its all India character. I am directed by the President of the Board to request such associations as have expressed their inability to participate in this year's championships to reconsider their decision and to extend their full co-operation and support as hitherto in the successful conduct of the championships.[43]

Even when the Board finally managed to ban the Pentangular in January 1946, the tournament's popularity had not waned. Following the ban, there were repeated appeals to restart the competition. The empty stands at the Ranji Trophy matches, a plight that continues even today to plague the tournament, contrasted starkly with a 25,000-strong attendance at the Pentangular matches. The anti-Pentangular campaign, whatever its guiding motive, failed to achieve its ends, evident from the disappointment expressed over the lack of public support for the Ranji Trophy, even after the Pentangular was stopped in January 1946. That the Pentangular was missed sorely is evident from the following description by Berry Sarbadhikary:

> The 1948 C.C.I Zonal Quadrangular—really a Triangular this time with the partition-affected North combining with the South—was a disappointment in many ways. The Bombay cricket fervour appears to have subsided with the passing away of the communal Pentangular and now is only reserved for Test cricket. They still talk of the Pentangular with that sad touch in their voice, of the tradition that kept the Bombay cricket enthusiasts agog, and of a revival of the Pentangular as the only practical and effective step towards revitalising Bombay cricket. They point to the inability of the Ibrahims and Phadkars in attracting a handful of spectators for the Kanga league. They contend now that the communal virus is gone, the Hindu-Muslim-Parsi-Christian tournament can do no harm. Knowledgeable people in Bombay still tell me that a Pentangular even today would draw a crowd of 40,000. If that be so why don't even 4000 turn up for a tournament which includes all the best players in the country?[44]

However, the ghost of the Pentangular was not buried soon. Fissures within the Board, exposed by the Pentangular, were once again out in the open during the next major controversy which erupted in 1948–49. This controversy, discussed in the following chapter, pitted the Board President, A.S. De Mello, against India's stand-in Test captain, Lala Amarnath, and was one of the earliest contests between player power and officialdom in Indian cricket history.

8

The Pretender and the Prima Donna

The unseating of Mr. Anthony De Mello from the Presidentship of the Board of Control for Cricket in India marks the end of a virtual dictatorship. Gifted with unbounded energy, resource and enterprise as well as with many of the shinning [*sic*] and streamlined qualities of a high power salesman and showman, Mr. De Mello imposed his will on Indian cricket for the best part of twenty-three years. Unfortunately his lustrum was also characterised by a series of controversial decisions and actions. The existence of a dictatorship of this kind could have been possible only with the support and connivance of the majority of those who comprised the parent body of Indian cricket. And if a genuine desire exists for the advancement and welfare of the game in this country, every effort must be made to free the Board of Control of gentlemen with too many irons in the fire of sport and commerce.[1]

If asked to rank the controversies that have plagued Indian cricket over the years, the Amarnath–De Mello affair would certainly rank as number two, a notch below match fixing. It was as sensational as it could get, with the President of the Board of Control for Cricket in India, A.S. De Mello, preparing a list of 23 charges of indiscipline and misdemeanour against Lala Amarnath, who was then the country's stand-in captain— he led the side in Australia in 1948 and in the Tests against the West Indies in 1948–49. Of the 23 charges, the most startling was that Amarnath, also a selector along with P.E. Palia and M. Dutta Roy, had accepted a bribe of Rs. 5,000 from officials and cricket enthusiasts in Calcutta to include Probir Sen of Bengal for the fourth and fifth Tests against the West Indies.

It all started when, in an Extra-Ordinary General Meeting of the Board on 10 April 1949, the Board President, A.S. De Mello, charged Amarnath with serious breach of discipline and suspended him from playing any

representative cricket for India or for any province in India. In support
of the decision, De Mello, in an interview to the Associated Press of India
on 14 April 1949 declared that

> The Board, at its meeting on April 10, was unanimous in its decision to take
> disciplinary action against Amarnath and it did not consider it necessary to
> hear him any more or any longer, as it had before it plenty of evidence about
> the veracity of which the members had no doubt.[2]

He also asserted that the 'affair had caused him much disappointment'
because he had 'at the sacrifice of many great friendships'[3] brought
Amarnath back into Indian cricket after the disciplinary action against
him during the 1936 tour of England.

In retaliation, Amarnath went on the offensive, saying that he found
it strange that the Board had arrived at its decision without giving him
an opportunity to defend himself. He added that he was not going to
take it lying down and 'the country will soon know the other side of
the picture and will then be in a position to judge and decide as to
whether the charges framed against me are correct'.[4] He also said that
he had 'sacrificed and suffered much—not only financially but in friendship as well—out of devotion and loyalty to the Board and its President.'[5]
He asked that, in the interests of Indian cricket the Board should make
public the charges made against him. 'While I do not expect any favour
from the Board, I certainly hope they will play cricket.'[6] Amarnath found
strong support among the Bengal lobby, mainly in Pankaj Gupta who
declared that Amarnath's suspension had been singlehandedly pushed
through by De Mello, and that he (Gupta) had in fact spoken against
the motion, which, incidentally was not even on the agenda for the 10
April meeting.

> I yielded to none in the matter. I was not concerned with the merit of the
> case and the resolution at that stage but against the manner in which it was
> brought up and rushed through. Having spoken twice against the motion
> being placed on the agenda, I could not have been a party to passing of the
> resolution even as a matter of principle. It was indecent in my opinion to
> associate the Rs. 5000 purse with the inclusion of P. Sen in the Test side.
> To connect the purse with P. Sen's inclusion was the thought, surmise,
> inference, and conjecture of persons, who perhaps, for reasons best known
> to themselves, lost the balance of judgment and good behaviour.[7]

Upset at being challenged from within the Board, De Mello declared
in the *Times of India* of 10 May 1949 that it was time to show Amarnath
that even if most of the Board's officials did not bark the Board of

Control for Cricket in India 'did have a dog that could bark and bite when indiscipline in Indian cricket was concerned'.[8] He condemned Pankaj Gupta stating:

> Such rash statements are attempts at creating malice. The misdemeanour of Captain Amarnath last season was seen, heard, and known throughout the country. I therefore had to submit the whole matter to the Board and did so at the full meeting on April 10 in a thoroughly constitutional manner. Discussions, in which all present participated for quite two hours were cool and cordial. At the end of the discussions, I submitted the phraseology of the resolution, which was unanimously passed. I can categorically state that there was no request for any revision or vote.[9]

Earlier at a press conference held in the Governor's Pavilion of the Cricket Club of India on 4 May 1949, De Mello had issued a statement to the media in which the charges against Amarnath were explained in detail:

> Lala Amarnath's suspension from playing any representative cricket for India or for any province was the accumulated result of numerous acts of misbehaviour and indiscipline during the last season—acts, which culminated in his blatant interview to a Lucknow newspaper, scathingly critical of the Board and its President, A.S. De Mello.
>
> That was the gist of Mr. De Mello's explanations to representatives of the Press at a conference on Thursday afternoon in the Governor's Pavilion of the Cricket Club of India. The charges against the substitute skipper of India's Test sides for the series against the West Indies, together with all the correspondence relating to the unfortunate affair, were set down with exceptional detail in a statement, which was distributed to all present, and after this had been pursued, Mr. De Mello invited questions and provided enlightenment on numerous points which were put to him. Twenty-three separate charges have been levelled against Amarnath, and the full list has been sent to him, while copies, along with relative enclosures, have been forwarded to the Vice-Presidents, the Honorary Secretary and the Honorary Treasurer of the Board of Control for Cricket in India, as well as to all its affiliated associations.[10]

These charges, as reported in the *Times of India* alleged negligence by Amarnath in his duties as captain, as reflected in his failure to organise net practice in good time before the first three Tests, largely due to his having arrived late at the Test venues; a demand by him for additional payment as captain for his out-of-pocket expenses in entertaining friends in his Delhi hotel; his last minute decision not to captain the states XI against the West Indies; his failure to notify the Board President of the injury that subsequently became a handicap to him and India in the second Test; his indisciplined utterances against the Board and its President at receptions and to the press; his insulting disregard of the Board in not replying to two letters sent to him; and finally, his illegal acceptance of a purse of Rs. 5,000 on the promise to include Probir Sen in the last two Tests against the West Indies.[11]

In response to these charges, Amarnath, on 5 June 1949 addressed a press conference at Calcutta where he distributed to the members present a 39-page, 27,000-word statement in an attempt to prove that De Mello was out to settle personal scores against him. In this booklet, he replied to each of the 23 charges and also stated that he knew that the Board, in effect, De Mello, would not rescind or revoke the decision, nor make amends for the grave injustice done to him or to the interest of sport in general. Commenting on Amarnath's statement, the *Sunday News of India* noted:

> Amarnath has adopted the simple expedient of emulating M. Molotov as a convenient refuge from the numerous misdemeanours, which have been attributed to him. All he has said is a categorical 'No' even in regard to utterances, which are alleged to have been made in the presence of a large gathering. According to Amarnath, his reported interview to a newspaper correspondent at Lucknow was a complete fabrication, the product of fertile imagination, though he has not bothered to suggest what could have been the object of the person responsible, one, more over, who was obviously most sympathetic towards him. If one were to take Amarnath seriously, he would be left aghast at the injustices heaped upon his devoted head and the enormity of the conspiracy of which he is supposed to be the innocent victim. And, since everything can be placed at Mr. De Mello's door, according to our blameless and long suffering substitute Test skipper, what could be more natural than a vigorous resort to mud slinging by the unfortunate aggrieved. Amarnath has tackled this in a really big way, with the quiet efficiency of a connoisseur, ignoring nothing that could smirch the antecedents of his accuser.
>
> To characterise this squabble between Amarnath and the President of the Board of Control for Cricket in India as an unfortunate affair, is, actually, an under statement. It has done the game in this country irreparable harm; and much of the responsibility for a most regrettable situation can be traced directly to the parent body, as well as to Mr. De Mello himself.... Those responsible for this ridiculous paradox will probably attempt to explain it away by declaring that the Beaumont Committee had, to all intents and purposes, exonerated Amarnath, and that subsequent honours extended to him were by way of reparation. Such an assertion would lead to the inference that the Board of Control are incapable of making an appropriate choice for key positions and that they ultimately display little confidence in their own judgement, as well as that of their nominees. For one reason or another, the

swashbuckling Amarnath has been pampered by Mr. De Mello as well as by the board ever since the first incident (his sending back in 1936), and now he has struck back at one, who himself claims to have been his benefactor.

Dignity is the guiding influence for the controlling bodies of all cricket playing countries in the world, but it does not appear to carry the same importance for the Board of Control for Cricket in India. When Amarnath was unceremoniously sent back to India thirteen years ago, he sobbed out his misfortunes during a railway journey to his port of embarkation. He has matured quite a lot since then. Now, instead of weeping at his suspension from Indian cricket, he has thrown out a veiled threat of legal action against the Board. That was all that remained to complete the effect of a thoroughly reprehensible business.[12]

In response to the charge that accused him of demanding additional payment for himself, Amarnath declared that he had asked for Rs. 150 for each Test player for eight days' stay at Test centres, which he thought was a perfectly legitimate request. He also strongly denied the allegation that he had accepted an illegal purse in Calcutta, saying that he had only accepted Rs. 5,000 from A.N. Ghose, Honorary Secretary of the Cricket Association of Bengal, as a contribution to the Amarnath Testimonial Fund—ironically, a scheme mooted by De Mello for Amarnath's benefit in 1947 when, in the interest of Indian cricket, Amarnath had cancelled his professional Lancashire League contracts and turned his back on the prospect of a contract with Sussex. In his own words, 'The Board, on Mr. De Mello's initiative, had decided to try and help me by reimbursing me partially (for the losses sustained).' As for De Mello's aspersion that Amarnath had taken money to include Sen in the team, Amarnath dismissed it as a figment of the Board President's imagination, pointing out that he alone could not have got Sen into the side without the consent of the other selectors, Palia and Dutta Roy. In that case, he asked, why had De Mello not drawn up a charge sheet against Dutta Roy and Palia?

Responding to the accusation that he dropped out of the states XI match against the West Indies at the last minute, Amarnath replied that he had informed the Secretary of the Board eight days before the match. Further, he stated that the decision on his participation did not rest with him but with his employer, the Maharaja of Patiala. About his alleged unwillingness to reply to the Board's letters dated 8 January and 21 February, he said that he had responded to them on 14 January and 7 April respectively. He ascribed the delay in replying to his various preoccupations following the three months he had had to devote to cricket, and to his foot operation in Kanpur.[13]

The *National Standard*, in an unprecedented move in world sporting history, published each of Amarnath's responses to De Mello's charges in 19 separate parts. The 19th or the last rejoinder went thus:

I deny 'continued insulting disregard of the Board'

Mr. De Mello's charge number 21

Your continued insulting disregard of the Board by not replying to our first letter dated the 8th January 1949, and yet another letter dated the 21st February 1949, as given hereunder which was sent to you, 'registered-ack-due' and which was duly received by you on the 24th of February 1949.

Dear Captain Amarnath,

I returned to Bombay early this week and was surprised that there was no reply from you to my letter sent to you through the kindness of Mily, Secretary to H.H. Maharajadhiraj of Patiala dated 8th January 1949. To avoid unpleasantness and other difficulties I would appreciate a reply to reach me at the above address before the end of this month. There is also another inquiry to make. In a speech made by you after the fifth Test match at Bombay you have referred to 'power politics' by the Board. Will you explain what you meant by the remark?

Captain Amarnath's reply

I totally deny Mr. De Mello's charge of 'continued insulting disregard of the Board.' I did reply to his letter of 8th January on the 14th of January—if you will look up its copy in reply to charge No. 17. I replied to Mr. De Mello's letter of 21st February on 7th of April, which, Mr. De Mello states was received by him on 11 April that is the day after the meeting that suspended me. The delay in replying to Mr. De Mello's letter (i.e. of February 21) was owing to my various preoccupations after the considerable time I had to devote to cricket for three months. My foot also had to be operated upon in Kanpur and besides I was positive I had replied to Mr. De Mello's letter of January 8 on January 14, which would have served to inform Mr. De Mello on the points he had raised.

Mr. De Mello's charge number 22

Your interview to the *National Herald* dated 2 April 1949 charging me personally, the Selection Committee and the Board with intrigue against you.

Captain Amarnath's reply

I deny categorically that I granted any interview to the *National Herald* or authorised its Editor or anyone else to publish any story quoting me. I possess conclusive documentary evidence to show that no interview could possibly have been given to the *National Herald* for publication on or about 2 April. This will also be borne out by the fact that as soon as my alleged interview to the *National Herald* came to my notice, I, under a registered letter, acknowledgement due, dated 4 April wrote to the Editor of the said journal contradicting the alleged statement that I had granted the interview. You will note that on 4 April when I denied giving the alleged interview I had no idea that there was any motion to suspend me on the 10th. I thus acted in good faith in writing the letter of contradiction. The question, therefore, of my charging Mr. De Mello personally, the Selection Committee and the Board with intrigues against me, does not arise for the simple reason that I have never made any such charges.

Mr. De Mello's charge number 23

Your speaking disparagingly to all and sundry about what transpired in the Selection Committee thus depriving India of the best efforts of selected players.

Captain Amarnath's reply

It is absolutely untrue that I spoke disparagingly to anyone about what transpired in the Selection Committee. Mr. De Mello should at least remember that he himself often evinced keen interest in the proceedings of the Selection Committee meeting with such questions to me as 'How on earth could so and so be chosen and how could so and so be dropped?' My uniform reply was, 'The Selection Committee did it. Don't ask me.'

It is amazing that Mr. De Mello should bring this charge against me. I was a selector along with the Nawab of Pataudi and Mr. V.M. Merchant in England in 1946 and again in Australia. Not one word was ever spoken against me on those occasions nor until the end of the West Indies tour. I have always known my responsibilities in the matter but Mr. De Mello must have his own good reasons to have preferred such a vague and frivolous charge. I have nothing more to say.

Patiala, 26 May 1949.[14]

Following the publication of his 27,000-word rejoinder, public opinion was deeply divided over whom to support, and there was conjecture that De Mello's enemies within the Board would use the opportunity to oust him from his position of Board President. Expressing this sentiment, the *Sunday Standard* of 3 July 1949 reported that 'there is no question that Bengal and Madras thinks alike on the Amarnath affair' and is determined to expel De Mello from the ranks of the Board. It went on to declare, 'There is every indication that the suspension of Amarnath is going to be made the medium of a very big gamble for the control of Indian cricket.'[15] De Mello, however, showed no signs of relenting and issued the following statement against Amarnath soon after his return from England after a two-month tour:

> Amarnath's statement of June 4 from Calcutta is as apocryphal as all others that he has continued to make once he attained the exalted position of substitute cricket captain of India. Reading through it, I can only remark that it is difficult to escape the conclusion that he and his hired assistants in Calcutta, like the proverbial mountain, have laboured really hard and brought forth a mouse. His statement is a veritable tissue of suppressions, misrepresentations and inventions. My return to India today and this statement by me ring the bell for round 20 of this slanging match started by Amarnath and his advisers. I am not going to quote again that Amarnath did so and so at Delhi and Bombay and so on. I shall leave all that for the exhibition bout on July 31. But I shall again emphasise that the matter was given full consideration at our meeting on April 10 and a unanimous decision was made at a dignified and cordial meeting. I cannot understand how all this malice and wearisome wrangling have since crept in. I shall name the culprits responsible for all this in our meeting on July 31. I am hundred percent confident that the Cricket Control Board of India will not permit Amarnathism to make a paradise for indiscipline in Indian sport and may I add that the game is more than the player of the game. But the player is born of cricket and it is for the players to remember this responsibility to its spirit and tradition wherever they may be—fielding, batting, bowling maiden overs or giving maiden speeches. Rude behaviour and indiscipline is not usually a striking feature in the character of those whose prowess on the field of sports attracts the plaudits of the public and the adulation of the hero worshippers. I am headlined as the 'Board'. Benevolent despotism is exercised by all such controlling bodies and the Cricket Control Board of India has always acted similarly with cricket and cricketers at home. It is not yet known and realised that Indian cricket, which has attained international manhood under me (1928–49) is my second religion and that with my eternal vigilance on her behalf I shall not tolerate indiscipline or nepotism of any kind in her ranks.[16]

The situation was further complicated when Amarnath announced his determination to drag the Board to court:

> Lala Amarnath told the Press Trust of India today that he had made up his mind to take legal steps against the Board of Control for Cricket in India for his alleged wrongful suspension by the board on April 10 last as a last resort to vindicate his honour. Amarnath said that 'the court of law was the only place where I can get justice.' He said that he had already circulated his public reply to all those who counted in Indian cricket, and he felt that the statement of the President of the Board on his return from Europe characterising his reply as a 'tissue of suppressions, misrepresentations and inventions' showed clearly that the President in the name of the Board was persisting in defaming him nationally and internationally.[17]

Soon after his intention was made public, influential commentators like A.F.S. Talyarkhan started rallying against Amarnath, adding spice to the controversy. In his column, *Take it from me,* Talyarkhan argued:

Instead of threatening to go to court, Amarnath should boldly seek permission of the board to attend its next meeting. He should ask to be permitted to appear in person, answer questions and generally satisfy everybody that the charges against him are false. If he is so adjudged he should ask to be reinstated. This to my mind is the only thing he can do as a cricketer against whom action has been taken. To go to court will mean that Amarnath will have to prove malice on the part of the Board. I dare say that those who were present at the meeting, which penalised him, will become the defendants to the suit. I was representing a province at that meeting and I, therefore, will also become an accused. Very well, at least I am ready to stand up to the Lala's charges. Let him prove that my vote for suspending him was based on malice, enmity, ignorance, or that I voted without the facts before me. As an individual and as a representative of that Board meeting I accept the Lala's challenge. Let him proceed. I will need no lawyer to defend me.[18]

That the *Sunday Standard* of 3 July was correct about Bengal trying to use the controversy to oust De Mello from the Board is evident from the following report published in the *Times of India*:

Bengal's attitude towards Cricket Board meeting

Further to the annual general meeting of the Board of Control for Cricket in India the representatives of the Cricket Association of Bengal have been instructed to represent to the Board that the resolution, which was passed at the Board meeting on April 10, suspending Amarnath from playing cricket for India and any province in India was illegal and ultra vires and should be expunged from the minutes of the Board; and that the matter should be referred to either a board of arbitration or a committee of inquiry. On this issue the Bengal delegates will endeavour to prove and satisfy the Board that according to law and the constitutional position, the Amarnath case was decided in an irregular and contrary [manner] to natural justice, Amarnath should have been given a chance, and if his case is referred to a committee Amarnath should be given all opportunities to answer the charges. The very fact that this matter did not figure in the agenda of the meeting on April 10 was contrary to the rules and regulations of the Board itself.

The Bengal representatives will also represent to the Board that the insinuations and allegations that have been levelled against the Cricket Association of Bengal apropos the Amarnath case were not fair, and the Board should make suitable amends as regards this. Anyway, it appears that the Bengal representatives will attend the meeting with the sole object of creating a better atmosphere and that they will do everything in their power to bring about a solution in an honourable way to this deadlock.[19]

On the day of the Board meeting, the *Sunday News of India* reported:

> Well! That fateful annual general meeting of the Board of Control for Cricket in India will be held this morning at the Cricket Club of India, and before another couple of days are over we will probably know whether those who are entrusted with the destinies of the game in this country have succeeded in extricating themselves from what can be considered as nothing better than an appalling mess. This mess revolves around the suspension of Amarnath and enough has been said on the subject to obviate further comment. According to a press report, Amarnath has sued the President of the Board of Control, Mr. A.S. De Mello, for defamation claiming a lakh of rupees as damages, and this suit will be heard at Calcutta, where the Lala evidently commands a great deal of support. It has also been stated that India's substitute Test skipper intends to drag the Board of Control itself into the Madras High Court after today's meeting.
>
> So if we accept Mr. De Mello's statement regarding his many kindnesses to Amarnath, it seems that the President of the Board of Control has sown the wind and now reaps the whirlwind. There have been so many conflicting stories about the attitude of the various affiliated Associations that it is impossible to anticipate anything definite from the deliberations at today's meeting, but we do hope that those who attend in a representative capacity are empowered to express views and make decisions on behalf of their sponsors, and that whatever they do at the meeting will be duly implemented by their principals.[20]

In the fateful Board meeting on 31 July 1949, a compromise was reached, which, in hindsight can be best described as a temporary truce. It was arrived at after Amarnath had tendered a qualified apology to the Board and its President. However, it was certainly a defeat for the Board, for the Board was forced to concede that its decision against Amarnath was *ultra vires* as no proper notice had been given and also as Amarnath had been given no opportunity to be heard. As a result, the Board was forced to delete the relevant portions from the minutes of the 10 April meeting.[21]

That the animosity between De Mello and Amarnath had not been buried even after the compromise of 31 July was evident from a statement Amarnath made in an interview prior to his departure for England in April 1950. In an interview to the *Times of India* before leaving to play for Lancashire, he said:

> De Mello has done me a lot of harm. But my reputation has been fully vindicated by no less a celebrity than Bradman in his memoirs. He had tried to drive me out of cricket, but without success. One day soon, I feel sure, he will come crawling to me, begging me to help him once again.[22]

He concluded saying:

> They came in large numbers to give Hazare, Mankad and Umrigar a grand
> send-off when they sailed from Bombay a few days ago. Don't they know
> that I am also going to play in the Central Lancashire league? But, anyway,
> they will gather in their thousands to greet me on my return after the
> successful season that I anticipate for myself with the same club that Worrell
> served as a professional last year.[23]

Something of the sort did happen a year later, when, to quote the
Times of India, 'De Mello was unceremoniously bundled out of the
Board of Control for Cricket in India'.[24] The Bengal lobby, led by Pankaj
Gupta and supported by Amarnath accomplished this coup, unseating
De Mello who had dominated Indian cricket for the best part of 25 years.
Commenting on De Mello's defeat, the *Times of India* stated, 'Unfor-
tunately the proceedings of the meeting seem to indicate that the oc-
casion was used as an opportunity for the settling of old scores and that
personal animosity played a big part.'[25] The correspondent concluded
saying:

> Indeed, the virtual cataclysm engulfed not only Shri De Mello but also some
> of those who had hitched themselves prominently to his chariot. Far from
> sympathising with the victims, I am glad that a salutary example has been
> made of one who sought to ride rough shod over the real interests of Indian
> cricket, as well as, of those who furthered their own ends by trailing along
> with him, but I am sorry that the general clean up that characterised the
> Board's twenty-second annual general meeting did not prove to be more
> comprehensive in its effect.[26]

As a rude reminder to De Mello that he was no longer in power,
Amarnath soon notified the Board that he was fit to play for India again,
a statement that received widespread media coverage.[27]

However, the battle had not been finally won for Amarnath. De Mello
did plot a comeback the next year, an attempt that marks the final phase
of this dirty affair.

Bundled unceremoniously out of the Board of Control, A.S. De Mello,
like all other dictators, was thirsty for revenge. For that he needed to
successfully outmanoeuvre the Pankaj Gupta–J.C. Mukherjee–Lala
Amarnath combine in the 1952 elections. Nursing the ignominy of
humiliation and insult, that's just what De Mello, astute politician that
he was, tried to achieve. Modern-day electoral campaigns with all their
dirty power play would have learnt much from the final episode of the
De Mello–Amarnath affair. Buying and selling of votes was common,

as was the use of muscle power. In return for votes, both sides held out the lure of lucrative administrative posts, including managerial positions of touring Indian teams. Both sides portrayed themselves as avenging angels, intent on righting wrongs done to Indian cricket during the other's tenure.

That De Mello had done much to develop cricket in India was beyond doubt. He had contributed to the building of stadiums and clubs, had organised tours and, above all, was instrumental in the establishment of the Board in December 1928. He used all these achievements to good effect in trying to regain his position. A section of the local English press was all praise for De Mello. In fact the *Times of India* once reported that 'all that stood to the credit of the parent body was the handiwork of De Mello and the new office bearers would find it extremely difficult to emulate him.'[28] Some leading sports journalists, close associates of De Mello, were critical of Gupta and Amarnath. Class and social status had suddenly turned important and De Mello's polish was preferred to the rusticity of Gupta and Amarnath.[29]

With the elections round the corner, De Mello was the favourite to win back the hot seat. Expressing this view, the sports correspondent of the *Times of India* reported on 12 October 1952:

> As anticipated the battle of the Presidentship had developed into a clash between the Bengal clique and that which supports my old and respected friend Anthony De Mello, and so well had the latter conducted his campaign that as late as on the day before the meeting there was a strong feeling evident that Mr. J.C. Mukherjee would certainly be dethroned by the veteran administrator he himself had unseated.[30]

Confident of victory De Mello had in fact arranged for celebrations at a leading Calcutta hotel. This too was reported by the correspondent of the *Times of India*, 'I am told that a wonderful celebration had been arranged at Calcutta's leading hotel in anticipation of that ostensibly happy event.'[31]

Indeed De Mello's task was easy in the absence of Pankaj Gupta who was away in England for the most part of September with the touring Indian team. Gupta was back in Calcutta in October, a couple of weeks before judgement day, and it was then that the final countdown began. Amarnath had a special role in the drama and his selection as captain for the forthcoming tour of Pakistan had much to do with the determination of keeping De Mello out. Commenting on the selection, the *Times of India* reported, 'Like a prima donna who bows numerous farewells Lala Amarnath comes back and forth as India's captain. That is no reflection

on him but on the pinchbeck Caesars of the Cricket Board of Control who
unlike Caesar's wife never seem above suspicion.'[32] It was also suggested
that, 'the motivations which excite the choice of India's captain are many
and mysterious. And the selection committee appears to change its mind
as often as a Hollywood actress changes her husband.'[33] It was justly
questioned why, six months after Amarnath had been discarded (he was
dropped for the tour of England in the summer of 1952), he was suddenly
invested with the duties of captaincy against Pakistan. It appeared out-
landish because Amarnath had done nothing in the intervening period to
merit selection, leave alone become captain.

The offer of captaincy had brought the Bengal clique closer to
Amarnath and it was with his support that they prepared themselves to
bring De Mello down for one last time. It was not without reason that
the *Times of India* asserted:

> There can be no doubt that the question of captaincy would play a big part
> in the ultimate result of the elections. No logical or practical explanation is
> possible in justification of the Board of Control's decision to dig Lala
> Amarnath from virtual obscurity and entrust him with the leadership of our
> representative side.[34]

That it was a tactical masterstroke was proved when on the morning
of the annual general meeting, the Bengal clique was assured of a
majority. Though the margin, 12:11, was as narrow as it could get, it
was enough to keep De Mello out of the Board. Realising the
implications of the defeat, De Mello ultimately withdrew his candidacy,
giving up his bid to regain the Presidency of the Board. It was poetic
justice. The very methods used by De Mello to become President and
remain in the post for over five years had now been used with finesse
to his detriment. That this was largely the handiwork of Pankaj Gupta
was evident from a report in the *Times of India*:

> Tony's adherents, however, had reckoned (they would win) without that
> incorrigible pan chewing diplomat Pankaj Gupta, who, with his customary
> thoroughness and resource had utilised the appallingly few days since his
> return from England to such excellent purpose that on the morning of the
> AGM the Bengal clique was assured of a majority.[35]

In hindsight, the saga of De Mello's ouster seems to have been
orchestrated with poise by Gupta and Amarnath. It was all part of a
meticulous plan, apparent from the tenor of Amarnath's statements to
the media a few months earlier, when he was forthright in declaring that
he would captain the team to England in the summer of 1952. That

particular ambition may have gone unfulfilled, but Amarnath was back in favour for the series against Pakistan. His outrageous statement about captaining the side led the sports correspondent of the *Times of India* to assert:

> I have no hesitation in saying today that if the parent body succeeds in disproving that its choice of a skipper was engineered by the exploitation of party politics, as usual, the only conclusion that can be drawn is that it is hopelessly inept and unschooled in its duties.[36]

Another surprise result of the election was the defeat of Colonel C.K. Nayudu. The overriding need to oust De Mello led the Bengal lobby to support H.L. Malhotra of Delhi against Nayudu for the post of Vice-President, and Ramaswamy of Madras for a seat on the Selection Committee. Colonel Nayudu's services were forgotten in a hurry and unworthy men rewarded for their loyalty instead.[37]

To add insult to injury, the Board headed by J.C. Mukherjee, decided to appoint De Mello chairman of the committee entrusting him with the arrangements for the celebration of the Board's silver jubilee. Unsurprisingly, De Mello declined to accept the post. In a letter to the Secretary of the Board he stated, 'As one of the founders of the Board of Control for Cricket in India I wish the silver jubilee celebrations great success but regret that owing to the uncertainty of my plans I am unable to accept your invitation.'[38]

This letter, written to stave off further humiliation, marks the end of De Mello's career as a leading Indian cricket administrator. His end was inglorious, and the ordinary Indian cricket fan of today hardly remembers his many achievements—among them the establishment of the Asian Cricket Confederation in 1948. It was no great surprise then, that De Mello's birth centenary, in 2000, was allowed to pass unnoticed by the Board. Except for a function organised by the Cricket Club of India, nowhere else was the occasion officially marked, or functions organised in his honour.

Soon after his defeat, it was suggested by some that De Mello had brought his downfall upon himself. However, the *Times of India* of 13 October 1932 rightly summed up the situation in the following words:

> De Mello could never have been able to pursue a dictatorial policy without the expressed or tacit approval of his fellow councillors. Several of those who were instrumental in the rise of De Mello to the highest administrative position in Indian cricket are still on the Board. It is futile for them to make a scapegoat of their latest victim, for they can never succeed in absolving themselves of their share of responsibility for what they now condemn.[39]

9

Mankad's Folly

Gupta and Mukherjee, who had masterminded De Mello's ouster from the Board in 1951–52, were again in the news in the summer of 1952 for wronging Vinoo Mankad, undoubtedly the best all-round cricketer India had produced before Kapil Dev arrived on the scene in 1978–79. Playing for India at a time when the game's finances were far from healthy, Mankad had to play professional club cricket in England to earn a living, and it was this overseas assignment that was at the root of the fiasco.

It all started when Mankad wrote to the Board of Control for Cricket in India in November 1951 informing them that he had an offer to play as a professional for Haslingden Club in the Lancashire league the next season.[1] With India scheduled to tour England in the summer of 1952, Mankad's assignment as a professional was not looked upon with favour by the leaders of the Board. However, given his reputation, the Board would have found it impossible to drop him, and accordingly, he was asked to come down from England to attend the trials for the forthcoming tour. It was surmised that the Board knew Mankad would have to rescind his contract with Haslingden to come to India to attend the trials and that hence it was all a ploy by the Board to keep Mankad out of the tour party.[2]

Upon receiving the invitation, Mankad agreed to go to England on the condition that his selection would be assured—by no means an unjust demand from one of the world's top all-rounders and the country's leading cricketer. It seemed all the more reasonable because Mankad who was under contract with the Haslingden Club as a full-time professional, would have to forsake his only source of income to make himself available for the trials. Mankad proposed to the Board that he would play in all four Test matches while assisting his club during the rest of the tour.

At first, the Board responded with sympathy, urging him to join the trials and leading him to believe that his selection was a formality. However, in a volte-face it was decided at a meeting of the Board on 16 February 1952 that Mankad's services were not required for the forthcoming tour. During the meeting, one of the selectors decreed that Mankad was not special and Indian cricket had dozens of players of his calibre![3] Soon after Mankad was dropped from the Indian team, he was offered a coaching job by the Ceylon cricket authorities. When the Ceylon authorities had first sounded him out in 1951, Mankad had expressed willingness to take up the position after retirement.[4] Using the opportunity offered by the Indian Board's decision to drop him, the Secretary of the Board of Control for Cricket in Sri Lanka (BCCSL) declared,

> The visit of a number of leading foreign teams in the post-war period including the West Indies, the Commonwealth and Pakistan have given great fillip to the game in this country. Ceylon has abundant talents in her youth, and, if her promising ones are coached on the right lines, the island will reach top class in the game. The Board has now before it the offer from the West Indies batting wizard Everton Weekes, but, although negotiations on his terms have been going on for some months, no decision has been taken. The Board would very much like to engage the services of Mankad provided his terms are reasonable, considering he is one of the world's greatest all-rounders today.[5]

Commenting on the Board's decision to drop Mankad from the touring team to England, the *Times of India* said:

> The meeting decided that Vinoo Mankad's services, even if available for the four Tests in England this summer should not be utilized. Mankad, it may be recalled, captured thirty three wickets in the series of Test matches against England in India, which is one of the finest performances in Test cricket of all time.[6]

As there was much criticism of the Board's decision to drop Mankad, the President, J.C. Mukherjee, tried to justify the Board's actions in an interview given to the cricket correspondent of the *Times of India*:

> It was pointed out to me by Mr. Mukherjee that the proceedings of the Board's special meeting were incorrectly reported, and that, far from making any direct allusion to Vinoo Mankad, the controlling body had merely arrived at a decision on the policy that should be followed with regard to the tour as a whole. As experience had shown that much dissatisfaction and heart burning resulted when the services of players who were not actually in the

touring side were utilised for Tests and other matches, it was resolved that the selectors of the team for England should be directed not to choose players who were not available for the entire tour. Thus since Vinoo Mankad had already intimated to the Board that his renewed agreement with a club in the Lancashire league for the coming season would make it impossible for him to assist the Indian touring side, it was obvious that the famous all-rounder could not possibly figure in the coming Test series against England. Much is being said by people who claim to be in possession of first hand information about the controlling body's refusal to meet Vinoo's demands in respect of an adequate guarantee and financial terms, but Mr. Mukherjee gave information that strenuous efforts had been made to ensure Vinoo's participation in the tour.[7]

But as fate would have it, Vijay Hazare's team faced disaster at every step in England. The situation was further complicated by Mankad's grand showing for Haslingden in the Lancashire league. In his first appearance for Haslingden, Mankad was unbeaten on 71 in a score of 118-5,[8] and even before the start of the first Test at Leeds, 5–9 June 1952, Hazare was forced to turn to Mankad for assistance. This was after two players, Ghulam Ahmed and Dattu Phadkar, got injured creating panic in the team. However, their injuries were not serious enough to justify the consternation and it was almost certain that both players would be fit for the first Test. Even if they were not, Chandu Sarwate and Ramesh Divecha, both part of the touring side, were available for selection. Given these circumstances the SOS sent by the team's management to Mankad was awkward to say the least. The *Times of India* summed up the situation in these words:

> Since last Saturday, when it became known that Vijay Hazare had cabled for the Board's permission to utilize the services of Vinoo Mankad in all the Tests, the sole topic of discussion among sports circles in Bombay appears to be the justification, or otherwise, of the touring skipper's action, an action which, it now transpires, has the full support of the team's manager Pankaj Gupta. Many are of the opinion that Hazare was driven to this recourse by the rapidly developing panic, which has engendered in him a premonition of defeat in the forthcoming Tests and the loss of prestige he feels he would suffer as a consequence. Others are definite that the Indian skipper was compelled to make this appeal by Pankaj Gupta, who, basing his calculations on what has happened thus far, is seriously alarmed at the disastrous effect an early defeat in the series would exercise on already unpromising gate receipts. This view is strengthened by the report that Gupta actually put through a telephone call to the President of the Board pressing for the desired sanction. The manager of our representative side has even gone to the length of impressing upon cricket authorities in England the fatal consequences an

appreciable loss on the present tour would impose on the future of the game in this country.[9]

It concluded saying:

> With the injuries of the two stalwarts in question not serious enough to necessitate their absence from the Leeds match, the question (of including Mankad) should never have been allowed to arise, and we would have been spared a great deal of embarrassment if the whole affair had been handled in the appropriate manner.[10]

In another report, the special correspondent of the *Times* criticised the BCCI and the manager of the touring team, Pankaj Gupta, stating:

> I can find excuses for the skipper of the side, for, as I have always maintained, he has not been fortunate enough to receive the specialized grooming for the important position that has been entrusted to him by a notoriously inept parent body, but it is impossible for us to be tolerant with Pankaj Gupta for the part he has played in the creation of an appalling mess, nor can we condone the completely weak kneed attitude of the President of the BCCI, Mr. J.C. Mukherjee, who had the power to put a stop to all the nonsense that was brewing and yet did not exercise it.[11]

It condemned Mukherjee saying that, 'the President of our parent body could have scotched the whole move decisively by ordering Gupta to carry on with the players under his charge. Instead of doing this Mr. Mukherjee readily afforded him all the encouragement he sought.'[12]

What made the actions of Gupta and the BCCI look worse was the demand that Mankad be released by Haslingden not just for the first Test but for all four Tests of the series. As the *Times of India* remarked:

> Vinoo Mankad should have been a certainty for this tour, but for reasons best known to the Board of Control for Cricket in India he was not included in the touring side. Furthermore, any question of his services being utilised in the Tests was placed completely beyond the bounds of possibility by a resolution passed by the parent body to the effect that only those players who were available for the entire tour would figure in the Tests. It is extraordinary that Pankaj Gupta, who was one of the most fervent supporters of the resolution, should have taken the lead in a move, which is intended to make a farce of it. Whereas the Board of Control for Cricket in India should have treated Hazare's cabled appeal for sanction to play Vinoo in all the Tests with the utter contempt that it deserved, the parent body has actually circulated it to all its affiliated associations and sought their reaction. And Bombay, with an alacrity, which should arouse interesting speculations and conjectures, was the first to signify its assent to the Indian skipper's request.[13]

It went on to state that Vijay Hazare's request for Mankad's reinstate-
ment was a direct betrayal of his obligations to the team and was 'worthy
of the severest censure'.[14]

On its part Haslingden Club was apprehensive about releasing Mankad,
knowing fully well that it would affect both the club's championship
prospects and its revenues. Accordingly, it refused permission and India
were forced to play the first Test match without Mankad—a match they
lost by seven wickets.[15]

However, before the start of the second Test, the Club, under intense
pressure reversed its decision. The *Times of India,* unclear about the
reasons behind the reversal asserted, 'Pressure of a very ponderous
variety has been exerted for the accomplishment of the end that has been
achieved, and the importunities of the manager of our team, Pankaj
Gupta may have had a great deal to do with that influence.'[16]

The release, it was surmised, may have been facilitated by Sir Herbert
Merett, a leading South Wales industrialist and President of the Glamorgan
County Cricket Club, who made a cash offer to Haslingden to release
Mankad. This, he mentioned, was to demonstrate to the Indians how
much Welshmen admired their pluck as cricketers.[17]

It is interesting to note that even when Mankad was being urged to
join the team, the BCCI did not take the initiative in arranging for his
release and had it not been for Sir Herbert Merrett, it may not have been
possible at all. Merret's gesture, the *Times of India* reported, was received warmly by the manager of the touring Indian team, Mr. Pankaj
Gupta. 'This is a very fine gesture and one which we expect from Wales,
where we have many friends. We want Mankad for all the remaining Tests
and I have told the Haslingden Club that we want him without any
special conditions being imposed.'[18] However, when confronted with an
agency message from London containing Gupta's statement, Mr. J.C.
Mukherjee, President of the BCCI, expressed ignorance regarding such
attempts to enlist Mankad's services. Referring to the overseas agency
message from London that Sir Herbert Merrett, President of the
Glamorgan County Cricket Club, had made a cash offer to Haslingden
Club with the hope of facilitating the release, Mr. Mukherjee felt that
such a move would not be appreciated in India and that the Board would
most likely refuse to have Mankad on those conditions.[19] Asked for an
opinion on the issue Mankad told the press, 'I shall be very pleased to
play for my country if I am asked, but as before, I am leaving the matter
to the Indian authorities and the club.'[20]

Against Mukherjee's wishes, Mankad was included in the team for
the second Test, with Haslingden consenting to release him for the rest

of the series. Commenting on the Club's gesture, the *Times of India* declared:

> Vinoo Mankad's unconditional release by Haslingden for the remaining three Tests doubtless must have provoked a great deal of jubilation in this country among followers of the game to whom inspiring results are essential to the proper appreciation of ventures of the kind in which the Indian team is now engaged, for the value of so competent an all-rounder to any side is unquestionable. The Lancashire league club's gesture to Indian cricket will go down in the annals of the game as one of the most generous on record.[21]

This match, one India lost by eight wickets, is still best known as Mankad's Test for the way he stamped his class on it from the outset. He scored 72 and 184, and also took five for 196 in the first innings. Even after this performance, however, the BCCI did nothing to honour Mankad and he was forced to return to Haslingden later in the month. The Club, reports declared, wanted to give him a hero's welcome, but Mankad, disappointed by the BCCI's treatment, turned down the offer of a red carpet reception.[22] As T.B. Hargreaves, Mayor of Haslingden said, 'We would dearly have liked to accord Mankad some civic reception, but we are respecting his wishes that no fuss should be made.'[23] Haslingden, he went on to add, was proud of Mankad for placing the town on the cricket map, and his performances, the Mayor hoped would help attract industrial investments to the town, which was one of the worst hit by the slump in Lancashire's cotton industry. Mankad's signing had increased the Club's membership to nearly 1,400, a record for the Club. Commenting on the issue, T.O. Lees, the Secretary of the Club said, 'Waiting for Mankad on the side board in the parlour of his home are scores of congratulatory letters and telegrams. We shall leave it to the crowd at Ramsbottom to give him the reception he deserves.'[24] Later in 1952, Ronald Aird, the Secretary of the MCC, singled out Mankad's performance against England as the performance of the year while addressing the country secretaries at their annual meeting at Lords.[25]

Back in India, the *Times of India* expressed disgust at the manner in which the BCCI and the team management—especially the latter—had conducted themselves on the Mankad issue:

> Principles have gone by the Board, solemn decisions which were based on the experience of past tours have been blithely ignored, and the manager of our side has not only condescended to accept for Indian cricket what is tantamount to pity and charity but also, to all intents and purposes, demanded that consideration. There is no doubt that the lack of wisdom and

incompetence displayed in this affair has gone far towards jeopardising our position in international cricket. Although there has been an outcry for another competent player, what our team in England really needed was another manager.[26]

Responding to this criticism, Gupta condemned the role of the Indian press in the entire issue. Pointing out that patriotism was nobody's monopoly, he declared, 'I have always had the prestige of the country in mind and despite whatever the Indian tinpot critics might say in the matter, I maintain that by bringing in Mankad I did not barter away India's prestige but enhanced it considerably.'[27] He also stated that,

> anyone who thought India would win in the Tests against England should have found a place in a lunatic asylum. If we could not beat the second English team under Nigel Howard on our home grounds, how could we, without Merchant, Amarnath and Mushtaq Ali, hope to succeed on a wet English wicket with the opposition at full strength?[28]

He concluded saying that as manager of the touring team he found it disheartening to receive anonymous letters from Indian supporters 'couched in impolite language'.[29]

As for Mankad himself, saddened by the shabby treatment meted out to him, he confirmed his decision to retire from Test cricket—an intention he first made public when he was dropped from the team at the end of the English season. Hearing this, the Board acted promptly, redeeming itself somewhat by persuading him to change his decision. The President, J.C. Mukherjee, conveyed this at a press conference held on 17 December 1952:

> Vinoo Mankad has decided to reconsider his decision to retire from Indian cricket. It will be recalled that some time ago Vinoo Mankad had declared in Ceylon that he would retire from Indian cricket. Vinoo is an outstanding cricketer and has still got a lot of cricket in him. It would be a great loss to Indian cricket if he ceased to play for India. I am very glad to say that he has, at my special request and that of some of his friends, agreed to reconsider his decision. It is indeed very good news for us that he has placed his services at the disposal of the Board.[30]

Mankad was finally felicitated on 23 December 1952 for having achieved the fastest double—100 wickets and 1,000 runs—in Test cricket, breaking the record of Monty Noble of Australia. He was presented with a purse of Rs. 12,501 in Bombay, an amount that reflects the state of cricket's finances in 1950s India. Commenting on this occasion, S.R. Tendolkar, the President of the Bombay Cricket Association deplored

Bombay's poor response to the appeal to raise a substantial fund for Mankad. This is evident from the following report published in the *Times of India*:

> Strong criticism of the sportsmanship of the Bombay crowds was made by Justice Tendolkar, who had sponsored the Vinoo Mankad fund. When Vinoo Mankad had completed the double on the third day of the second Test against Pakistan by dismissing Waqar Hassan after tea in Bombay, he sent around the hat, in appreciation of this record breaking feat on Sunday morning only to receive a niggardly response. The East stand was so tightly packed that it was impossible to make a collection, the North Stand contributed a sum of two hundred rupees and the Gymkhanas promised to make collections themselves from their members, but when the hat was passed around in the clubhouse of the Cricket Club of India one of the sportsmen there actually brushed it away and complained that he was being disturbed from watching the Test. The Club, however, made a handsome contribution later on.
>
> If the forty thousand spectators that were witnessing the game on that day had put in their mite, Justice Tendolkar continued, he would have been in a position to make a decent present to Vinoo Mankad. As it was, he had to make an All India appeal which resulted in his being able to hand over a cheque for Rs. 12,501. Of this amount the Madras Cricket Association had contributed Rs. 501, but although he had learnt that Bengal had started a fund of their own, they had not even cared to acknowledge his letter thus far.[31]

Compared to the niggardly response to the purse in the home of Indian cricket, Bombay, other regional centres responded with zest to the effort to honour the country's leading cricketer. While Justice Tendolkar received contributions from all over India, including distant parts of Bihar,[32] Mankad was fêted by the members of the Nagar community, to which he belonged, at a public function in which he was presented with a purse of Rs. 400 and a souvenir. Also, in what was a touching gesture, Mankad was greeted with a song written in his honour on this occasion.[33]

In recognition of his achievement, Mankad was also offered a coaching assignment by the Rajasthan Sports Club. Commenting on the value of this scheme, the cricket correspondent of the *Times of India* said:

> Vinoo, from all accounts, has worked wonders with the members of Haslingden, the League club by which he is employed in England, and I am confident that his efforts here will produce equally pleasing results. He has had the advantage of an excellent grounding in the game in Jamnagar, where in addition to his close association with some of the most famous personalities of the game, he was also coached by Bert Wensley, and the experience he

has gained in Test cricket makes him an ideal choice for the task entrusted to him. There was one department of the game on which Wensley laid particular stress, fielding. Vinoo Mankad, I know, has a similar outlook on the game, and if he succeeds only in turning out twenty exceptionally keen cricketers who appreciate the value of smart fielding and turn that knowledge to account he will have achieved what has very definitely not been done in this country hitherto.[34]

It is certainly ironic and even shameful that one of the greatest Indian cricketers was treated in such an irresponsible manner towards the end of his career. However, that this behaviour by the Board was no flash in the pan will be evident when we turn our attention to the umpiring fiasco that plagued Indian cricket through the 1950s.

10

Men in Black and White

It's like a cauldron in Test cricket and it is calculated to make the job of umpiring even harder.

Mervyn Kitchen, 1998.[1]

With cameras now making a compelling case for seriously limiting the power of on-field umpires,[2] it would be proper at this point to throw a glance at this rather 'endangered' and often controversial species in India. There is a nostalgic touch to much of this chronicle, not least because the most important yet most hapless figures on the cricket field are the two men in white coats. White coats, though, are vestiges of a hoary past and have been replaced by coloured shirts and silk ties in recent times with umpires even endorsing 'Fly Emirates' as part of modern cricket's commercial revolution.[3] Despite their importance in determining the outcome of cricket matches, umpires, on most occasions, remain in obscurity. Barring a few exceptions like Frank Chester,[4] Dickie Bird,[5] David Shepherd[6] and more recently Steve Bucknor,[7] S. Venkatraghvan[8] and Darrel Hair,[9] even the most ardent of cricket enthusiasts finds it difficult to name umpires of longstanding fame. Shepherd's hop,[10] much to the amusement of the crowd every time the score reaches Nelson, or Bucknor's nod before putting his finger up to send a batsman back to the pavilion may be modern cricket's enduring picture postcards, but such postcards are too few given the amount of cricket played and amount of time spent by the umpires in the middle. A list of legendary Indian umpires is non-existent with Swaroopkishan, the only umpire to be awarded the Padma Bhushan, standing tall as the lone patriarch.[11] While India has produced cricketers of world stature with alacrity, one often wonders why umpires have lagged behind. The answer, as will become evident, lies in the outrageous way umpires were appointed in India's cricketing past, a controversy glossed over in all existing works on Indian cricket. One of Indian cricket's worst controversies, it is time to bring it out of the closet.

In the years 1940–60, real trouble with umpiring in India did not arise due to a dearth of good umpires, but from a faulty and controversial method of appointing them.[12] Appointment of umpires for first-class matches was dependent solely on the whims of the secretaries of the State Cricket Associations. Secretaries sent the list of selected umpires to the BCCI. Accordingly, if the secretaries themselves were on the list, as was often the case, their appointment was assured. The best known Indian umpires of the 1940s and 1950s, M.G. Bhave of Maharashtra and Karmakar of Baroda, are examples of such selection. When a secretary was not a candidate, he invariably had a favourite who pipped the more qualified at the post. Men of merit were often victims of this corrupt system, never appointed to umpire important matches unless they curried favour with the appointing bosses. Prabhakar Balkrishna Jog of Maharashtra, who started his umpiring career in 1939 and stood in 400 or more regional matches spanning a long period of 20 years, was thus never allowed to umpire a Test match. In 1947, Jog and Bhave officiated in the prestigious David Cup final in Poona.[13] While Bhave soon became the first Maharashtrian umpire to do Test match duty, Jog was rarely given a chance to officiate in Ranji Trophy encounters. The reason behind this, as Jog mentioned during an interview with J.C. Mukherjee, the Board President, on 15 November 1952 at the Cricket Club of India, Bombay, was his refusal to pay Bhave half his remuneration after a Ranji Trophy match in 1948. The transcript of this interview was published by Jog in his book, *How's that? 'Board of Control' Out*:

> Jog: Coming to the point, Sir, I wish to let you know that great injustice has been done to me and I am not appointed as an umpire in any of the Test matches. Mr. Bhave and MCA of Poona do not recommend my name and hence I am not included in the panel of umpires.
>
> Mr. Mukherjee: How are your relations with Mr. M.G. Bhave?
>
> P.B. Jog: Sir, what should I say! Our relations are not good. They are strained. I have criticised him in my public lectures stating that Mr. Bhave is the sole dictator in the MCA and the MCA is a monopoly of Bhave and Co. When I earned about Rs. 300 by umpiring a Ranji Trophy match in the year 1948, Mr. Bhave asked (for) 50 per cent of my earnings from umpiring. I was asked to donate Rs. 150 to the MCA. He said that chances for umpiring are given due to the recommendation of MCA and hence I should pay 50 per cent of my earnings to the MCA. Sir, paying MCA means paying Mr. M.G. Bhave.

This proposal of Bhave I refused and so I am not recommended for any Test match.[14]

Drawing attention to the rampant nepotism in the appointment of umpires, the sports correspondent of the *Times of India* declared:

There can never be the slightest doubt that Bombay is outstanding among the regional cricket associations for the number and competence of its umpires. Yet, only one Bombay umpire J. Patel figures in the list of 18 that constitutes the All India panel, while Maharashtra has four representatives. Even humble Bihar has been honoured with three nominees in the list. Very significantly, Prabhakar Jog, who is by far the most experienced umpire in the whole of Maharashtra has not been included... for he has not only refused steadfastly to toe the Bhave line but also persisted with considerable effect to expose the extraordinary antics of my genial old friend and his obliging stooges and bully boys....[15]

On hearing Jog's complaints, J.C. Mukherjee advised him to meet A.N. Ghose, the Secretary of the BCCI. This meeting, held in room number 6 of the Cricket Club of India (CCI) on 15 November 1952, went on thus:

Jog: Are you aware of the fact that great injustice has been done to me by the MCA and Mr. M.G. Bhave?

Ghose: Yes, I can see that. You come through MCA.

Jog: How can I come through the MCA when Mr. Bhave and the MCA are against me? What am I to do under these circumstances? If you find me competent then alone you appoint me as an umpire for a Test Match. I want to prove my ability by giving any Test that you propose.

Ghose: Why don't you compromise with Mr. Bhave?

Jog: For what?

Ghose: So that he sends your name for inclusion in the All India Panel.

Jog: Where is the question of compromise? I must get my inclusion in the All India Panel on merit.

Ghose: True, but how can we displease Bhave?

Jog: The question of pleasing or displeasing Bhave does not arise. If other men like me, other than his friends deserve to be appointed an umpire, are you going to discard him?

Ghose: That is not the point. Look here Mr. Jog, there are certain things which cannot be discussed openly.[16]

Finally, Ghose asked Jog to apply directly to him and promised to redress the injustice.

Acting on his advice, Jog applied directly to the BCCI seeking an examination. The letter that he received from Ghose after giving him 'seven reminders' declared:

> Regarding umpiring I will place your letter before the umpires committee for their consideration and I will let you know their decision in due course. I will, however, once more request you to put your claims through the local Association, viz., the Maharashtra Cricket Association who should recommend your name for inclusion in the Ranji Trophy panel and also in the All-India panel of umpires.[17]

On receipt of this letter Jog met Bhave at the Maharashtra Cricket Association (MCA). The interaction between the two epitomises the nonchalance that characterised Bhave's attitude:

> Jog: I have received a letter dated 9th September 1953 from Hony. Secretary of the Board of Control for Cricket in India Shri A.N. Ghose and he asked me to put my claim through the Maharashtra Cricket Association. What have you to say now? When will you like to send my name to the Board as per the letter?
>
> Bhave: I will consult the umpiring committee of the MCA and then will let you know the decision.
>
> Jog: Did you consult them before you sent your name along with the names of Mr. B.J. Mohoni, A.R. Joshi and Nagarwalla?
>
> Bhave: No.[18]

Failing to break the ice, Jog met Ghose again on 16 November 1959 at Poona. This interaction turned out to be even more interesting:

> Jog: Sir, it is now exactly seven years that you have not done anything in the matter. I have been writing to you all these days and you have not replied to any of my letters though sent by registered AD.
>
> Ghose: Yes, it is a fact. I am sorry.
>
> Jog: On 10.3.57, I posted my leaflet 'I Challenge' but you have not expressed your views on the same. Here is my new book 'Mee Ha Asa Ahe'. Kindly go through the English portion—which directly refers to my umpiring and

the Board. Kindly go through the cuttings of the *Times of India*, which are put in the book.

Ghose: I thank you for the book and will go through it.

Jog: What is to be done about my umpiring? It is high time. Nearly 12 years have passed since I am agitating this point.

Ghose: Mr. Jog, we will have a special examination for you and we will appoint you in the Test match after you pass the examination.

Jog: I accept. Sir, but what about Mr. B.J. Mohoni, Mr. A.R. Joshi and Mr. Nagarwalla and Mr. M.G. Bhave? They have not passed any examination nor have they umpired like me continuously for a number of years. I say that the same rule should be applied to all. Why should there be any difference like this?

Ghose: Their names are already on the panel and now the question of examining them does not arise.

Jog: Who included their names on the panel? And how did they manage to come on the panel?

Ghose: Mr. Bhave did so in the year 1948, when he was the Hony. Secretary of the Board.

Jog: That is exactly what I am telling you for all these days. This type of their inclusion in the panel of umpires necessarily means favouritism and partiality. This is what I am opposing all these days. Partiality of this type is not expected in sports. Of course, I do not mean to say that you should do the same favour to me but on principle I strongly object to their inclusion and my exclusion when I am their contemporary. Anyway, I am ready to appear for the examination anywhere and at any time as per your directions. Is it not unfair to include the favourites directly?

Ghose: Yes, it is not fair.

Jog: Can you give me the list of umpires who are directly included?

Ghose: The list is not with me just now.

Jog: Kindly send it to me on your return to Calcutta. Also send me a copy of the Constitution of the Board.

Ghose: I will send it to you. You send the Judgement of the civil suit against Mr. Bhave.

Jog: I will definitely send the copy to you. [Jog adds as postscript that he sent a copy of the Judgement immediately to Mr. A.N. Ghose, which detailed the decree of Rs. 12,500 against Mr. Bhave].

Ghose: Well then Mr. Jog, you kindly apply to the Hony. Secretary who will let you know the decision, and inform you of the date of the special examination.

Jog: If you would have stated this in 1952, I would have by the time umpired a number of Test matches.

Ghose: I am sure Mr. Jog, you will pass the examination.

Jog: Excuse me, Sir, in such examinations we have not only to pass but get cent per cent marks, otherwise if the passing percentage is 40 per cent the umpire who passes with 40 per cent marks will ruin 70 per cent cricketers and as such mere passing is not the criterion.

Ghose: True, I agree with you entirely.[19]

On the basis of his discussions with Ghose, Jog applied to the Honorary Secretary for a date of the special examination. In fact, on the same day Jog met Mr. M. Chinnaswamy, the Secretary of the Board. The meeting, which took place on the terrace of Chinnaswamy's 'newly constructed bungalow', went thus:

Jog: Have you read all about the maladministration of the MCA?

Chinnaswamy: Yes. I have followed what you have to say.

Jog: Now coming to the issue of my umpiring, Sir, can you not directly appoint me as an umpire without the recommendation of the local authority?

Chinnaswamy: In ordinary course we may not. But in your case, we will definitely consider with a different angle.

Jog: By the way, did you see the crowd that attended my lecture yesterday?

Chinnaswamy: Yes, I was just passing by and I saw the huge crowd near the Club of Maharashtra.

Jog: This is how I expose Mr. Bhave and the MCA in public meetings.

Chinnaswamy: Yes, I have seen that.

Jog: Mr. Chinnaswamy, I am of the opinion that the monopoly of the group is always harmful to the progress of the game and it must be rooted out.[20]

However, as was the case in the past, all his appeals and correspondence went unanswered. He met Ghose for a third time in Poona on 18 November 1960. On this occasion, Ghose, guilty of his past actions, informed Jog that he would instruct Chinnaswamy, the Secretary, to do the needful immediately:

Jog: Sir, it is exactly after a year that we are meeting. What about my special examination?

Ghose: This time I will personally ask Mr. Chinnaswamy to do the needful.

Jog: You have not sent me the copy of the Constitution and have not returned the judgement copy sent to you. Similarly you have not given me the list of umpires who are directly included in the panel without any examination.

Ghose: I am sorry. I forgot to send it.

Jog: Is it a fact that all such directly recruited umpires are either secretaries of the various cricket associations or the friends of the secretaries?

Ghose: Yes, I think so.

Jog: This is highly objectionable. In my case, you are neither including me directly nor examining me. You are avoiding me. For the last nine years I am after you but on this count or the other you are postponing my appointment.

Ghose: This time I will certainly do something for you.

Jog: Mr. Ghose, I do not want your favour. Give me what I deserve. If you do not want me to be an umpire frankly tell me so but do not dodge.

Ghose: Don't get angry Mr. Jog. I will positively arrange for your examination immediately.

Jog: Have this new book, 'M.C.A: A Huge Fraud'. Kindly go through it and express your views if you like. You are trying my patience. Now at least examine me before the MCC comes or some foreign team comes to India so that I can umpire the Test match; otherwise after 50 you will say that I am age-barred.

Ghose: No, No, I will not let you down this time.[21]

Finally, Prabhakar Jog received a letter from Chinnaswamy on 31 October 1961. The letter, unpleasant as usual, asserted, 'Whether an examination should be held or not next year will be considered by the Umpires sub-committee. If it is decided to hold an examination for the

umpires you will be intimated. You can sit for the same when it is held.'[22]
It had, as is manifest, no reference to the special examination promised
by A.N. Ghose.

It is evident that the deciding factor in the appointment of an umpire
in India was favouritism; and knowledge, respectability and experience
were in most cases over-ridden by favouritism. Accordingly, it was not
without reason that the *Times of India* published the following report:

> British sportscribes covering the Tests were today taking the Indian umpiring
> to task for errors which have operated against both sides. The *Daily Herald*'s
> Ian Todd alleged that the two amateur umpires in Madras are well below
> the Test standard adding that several decisions backed this. Todd cited the
> instances of two appeals by Barry Knight, which were disallowed by an
> amateur umpire, and questions the lbw decision against Salim Durrani, who,
> he said, had certainly nicked the ball when given out. The *Daily Mirror*'s
> Clive Taylor said, 'There have already been six bad decisions. India is working
> on the system of one experienced Test umpire paired with a new boy.
> Ironically the bulk of the errors have come from the experienced man. Both
> sides are suffering. Once an appeal is made, the game becomes a lottery.
> Anything can happen.'[23]

Even in festival matches the issue of appointing umpires was fraught
with controversy. It was once declared that umpires would only be
appointed by the Board and they would be from among the Board's
panel of umpires. However, in a festival match at Poona on 21 December
1963, one of the umpires who officiated was not appointed by the
Board, nor was he a member of the Board's panel. He was a distant
relative of M.G. Bhave whose elder brother was also the Treasurer of
the MCA.

As a mark of protest against this corrupt system, Prabhakar Jog finally
resorted to a hunger strike in January 1964. However, even Gandhian
techniques proved futile; such was the dirt that had accumulated in
Indian cricket. Jog concluded his book with a letter addressed to the
multitude of Indian cricket fans, seeking justice and fairness that
remained elusive:

> I have put my case before you through this booklet. On going through it you
> will find that the Board has done great injustice to me. Right from 1948 I
> am requesting the Board authorities to appoint me as an umpire for the Test
> matches, but they have always turned a deaf ear to my requests. You will find
> from the correspondence that Mr. A.N. Ghose is mainly responsible for the
> injustice done to me; when there existed no umpiring examination for Test
> umpires he asked me to come through MCA, which was totally impossible

for me because I had strongly criticised the MCA. This fact Mr. A.N. Ghose positively knew when he was the Hony. Secretary of the Board for a number of years. He kept me waiting right from 1951 to 59. After 1959 he asked me to approach M. Chinnaswamy, who stated saying that I should pass the examination. When I offered myself for the same he purposely kept me in the dark. Though my contemporaries Mr. B.J. Mohoni, Mr. N.D. Nagarwalla, Mr. A.R. Joshi, Mr. N.D. Karmakar and the late Mr. M.G. Bhave were taken up directly on the panel of umpires without passing any umpiring examination of any sort I was dropped for the only reason that I was not a friend of any Secretary nor the Secretary. Thus in order to agitate the matter I started the hunger strike. I had written to Mr. A.N. Ghose and Mr. M. Chinnaswamy about my hunger strike but they have not cared to reply.[24]

11

Match Fixing
An Enemy of Yore

> I came to associate cricket in my own boyish and starry-eyed way with all
> that was good, noble and worthwhile. Today the game is spoilt, and spoilt
> rotten. The days of innocence have been gobbled up by sponsors and
> sodom. All over the cricketing world beastly people have made our time
> and the game we loved into nothing.[1]

Cricket to all its historians has quintessentially been the preserve of
'gentlemen'. Reports, surveys and commentaries during the match fixing
controversy were quick to declare unanimously that Hansiegate and the
stunning discoveries following it which reached a climax with the
Central Bureau of Investigation (CBI) report had signed a death warrant
to this noble, gentlemanly sport. It was this unabashed condemnation
of the modern that compelled me to think of the character of the sport—
not just in contemporary society, but in its historical evolution. Are these
'beasts' that Rudrangshu Mukherjee refers to in the quotation given
above, truly a product of our generation? Was cricket really ever a sport
far removed from the vices of politics and commerce? This entire volume
is an exercise which proves that there was always corruption and vice
in cricket. Indeed, history tells a different story, and it is important in
any analysis of cricketing controversies, that we recount a critical yet
different trajectory of the game, before we begin to compose the oft-
familiar jeremiad.

Corruption and vice in cricket may be traced back to the early 1740s.
S.M. Toyne establishes this fact in his *The Early History of Cricket*. He
writes:

> After the game had become fashionable in the 1740s betting rose to fantastic
> sums of one thousand pounds or more. Of one match it has been stated that

the side bets among spectators and players totaled twenty thousand pounds. In the early part of the nineteenth century the game itself was in danger of ruin since it had become the chief medium for national gambling. Bookmakers attended the matches, odds were called as the fortunes of the game fluctuated, and side bets on the score of individual players led to bribery and cheating. One noted player took hundred pounds to lose a match. Even the Hambledon club was said to have usually staked five hundred pounds on each match.[2]

Toyne chronicles contemporary disappointment at the sad plight of the game. For instance, one Miss Mitford lamented:

I anticipated great pleasure from so grand an exhibition. What a mistake! There they were, a set of ugly old men, white-haired and bald headed instead of our fine village lads with their unbuttoned collars, which gave an air so picturesque to their glowing bounding youthfulness, there they stood railed in by themselves, silent, solemn, slow-playing for money, making a business of the thing, a sort of dance without music instead of the glee, the fun, the shouts, the laughter, the glorious confusion of the country game, but every-thing is spoilt when money puts its stupid nose in ... so be it always when men make the noble game of cricket an affair of betting and hedgings and maybe cheatings.[3]

So, match fixing, which appeared in recent writings to be a young teenaged lad is in reality one of the oldest surviving 'gentlemen'. This phenomenon was not restricted to the subcontinent, but was a global affliction initially making its appearance in the very country that gave birth to the game.[4]

In India, one of the earliest known attempts to bribe a batsman into throwing his wicket away, as G. Rajaraman writes, 'was in 1935 in the Moin-ud-Dowla Gold Cup final between Freelooters, chasing a hat-trick that would give it the Cup for keeps, and Retrievers'.[5] Rajaraman goes on to declare:

Legend has it that Lala Amarnath, who later went on to lead India, was offered 10,000 rupees—a princely sum then—not to stand between Freelooters and the Gold Cup. He turned it down and made an unbeaten century against some hostile pace bowling by the West Indian Learie Constantine. Lala Amarnath apparently pointed out that the Maharaja of Alirajpur had not invited him to play for Freelooters and that he would not betray his own captain, the Yuvraj of Patiala.[6]

In the 1940s, for the first time in the history of Indian cricket a player was suspended for 'selling a match'. This match was played in Bombay in 1948 between Dadar Parsee Colony Sports Club and Brothers Club and was the penultimate match of the Kanga league.[7] In this match, J.B. Khot, the captain of the Dadar side was accused of 'fixing'. It was alleged that Khot, who had opened the batting and was unbeaten on 39, carrying his bat through in the process, deliberately wasted valuable time in the middle when his side was four runs short of an outright win. Eventually, they lost the match by 2 runs. This incident created a major furore in Bombay, more so because Khot, an established professional, had a great record for his club in the Kanga league. Commenting on the incident, A.C. Perreira declared in the *Sunday News of India*:

> There has been much heartburning among the pundits of the game at the disciplinary action taken by the Dadar Parsee Colony Sports Club against their Captain, J.B. Khot. From authentic information I have gathered, I am not in a position to state that Khot was in no way to be blamed for not securing the maximum number of points against Brothers Club in their last but one tie in the Kanga league. Khot himself told me Sunday last that if there was any intention on his part to sell the match, he could easily have thrown his wicket away. Instead, he was so keen on a victory that he went in to bat No. 1—a thing which he never usually does—and was unbeaten on 39 when stumps were drawn. The main ground for his suspension is that he is alleged to have wasted valuable time in the closing stages of the match when his team needed four runs for an outright win. But there is no blinking the fact that if he did so, it was because of circumstances beyond his control. Few are aware that his partner M.T. Rajkotwalla got a severe cramp and Khot did his utmost to relieve his colleague of the excruciating pain.
>
> To punish Khot therefore, because of one fall from grace is to ignore his previous great records as a captain not only for Dadar Parsee Colony SC but for other institutions as well. The Kanga league Executives should immediately look into the matter as the decision has been looked upon by trenchant critics as most inexplicable. I hope authorities will take cognizance of the drastic steps against the Provincial player and will give sufficient weightage to his past sportsmanship and not condemn him on a single incident for which action has been taken, not because his teammates resented it, but because the committee of his club did so.[8]

Against such a history, the CBI's comment following the match fixing controversy a few years ago that cricket as it is played now is not the game written about by Neville Cardus or played by Don Bradman, sounds extremely naïve. Also, denouncing globalisation as the agent of cricket's corruption is missing the trees for the woods. Economic liberalisation is a global trend, and to expect that cricket would be immune to it is a façile assumption. Rather, if cricket manages to shun its feudal codes and become truly professional—the forces of globalisation are expected to steer the game along that path—its codes will be clarified and so will be the punishments for breaching them. The CBI report bespoke of a commitment to stamp out corruption from the game in a manner hitherto unknown. We must recall that if the MCC managed to purge similar cankers from cricket 200 years ago, there is no reason to doubt that present-day administrators should be able to follow that precedent if their efforts are honest and rigorous.

Neither should we assume that the match fixing scandal is an isolated occurrence. The global history of sport, especially of games that arouse primal passion among audiences and therefore succeed in attracting huge corporate sponsors, is full of such instances.

And none of these scandals has ever threatened the existence of the game in the manner suggested by some Indian commentators. The match fixing episodes leading upto the 1919 Black Sox scandal in US baseball offer a striking parallel to the cricket controversy. A brief look at the commonalties between the two events should give hope to cricket enthusiasts that the reputation of the game is not beyond redemption. In 1919 the allegations against the Black Sox accused were based on circumstantial evidence, much like the accusations of match fixing against some Indian and international players. The baseball accused were freed by the judgement of 2 August 1921 due to lack of evidence. But the next day Commissioner Kenesaw Mountain Landes in charge of investigations unilaterally suspended the eight suspects including the legendary 'shoeless Joe Jackson'. The United States of America was emerging as a capitalist power in 1919, in much the same way as India today. Market forces and capital were making their presence felt with regard to most American sports, baseball being a prime example. Yet Landes managed to purge the lesions affecting baseball, despite the huge odds against him. His efforts have earned him a place in baseball's Hall of Fame.[9] Earlier last year, a clean World Cup in South Africa demonstrated that cricket administrators across the world are capable of achieving a similar feat.

12

All the Skipper's Men
The Ban of 1989

The 1989 controversy marks a watershed in the history of Indian cricket. This was the first time that the growing commercial prospects of the sport overtly asserted themselves in a tussle between the BCCI and the players. In this episode, it is possible to identify an intensifying professionalism, with the new trend pulling sharply against established structures. The 1980s had opened the eyes of both the erstwhile amateur and those at the head of official bodies to the fact that the nature of the game was fast changing. A growing commercialisation of the game was loosening older structures of dominance, and it may be assumed that it was this realisation that made commerce the crucial point of contest between the players and the BCCI, seen in its full venom in the recent contracts controversy that almost brought the cricket world to a standstill. From this time on, it became evident to all concerned that cricket was an emerging mass commodity, and issues central to the game, such as institutional control over the players as opposed to a measure of professional autonomy, began to be defined through a tussle over an independent claim to the trophies of commercialisation.

In a stunning move on 6 August 1989, the BCCI debarred six top Indian cricketers, Dilip Vengsarkar, Kapil Dev, Ravi Shastri, Arun Lal, Mohammed Azharuddin and Kiran More from playing international and domestic cricket for one year for taking part without official sanction in exhibition matches in the US and Canada after their tour of the West Indies in May.[1]

Six other members of the touring team—Sanjay Manjrekar, M. Venkatramana, Sanjeev Sharma, Ajay Sharma, Narendra Hirwani and Robin Singh, who had also undertaken the tour, were let off on grounds of inexperience with fines of Rs. 15,000 each. All the 12 players against whom the BCCI took the toughest action also forfeited the balance of Rs. 35,000 due to them for the West Indies tour.[2] The members of the touring party had initially received Rs. 30,000 as tour fee from the Board.

The ban was imposed at the conclusion of a two-day meeting of the Disciplinary Committee of the BCCI in Bombay on 5–6 August 1989. The Committee, which consisted of Mr. B.N. Dutta, the BCCI President, Mr. P.M. Rungta, Mr. M.K. Mantri, Mr. A.W. Kanmadikar and Mr. I.S. Bindra declared that:

> After considering the entire facts, circumstances, documents and papers, (the disciplinary committee) came to the unanimous conclusion that Dilip Vengsarkar, Kapil Dev, Arun Lal, Ravi Shastri, Azharuddin and Kiran More be debarred from any cricket conducted and authorized by the BCCI and its affiliated associations for a period of one year from August 6, 1989 to August 5, 1990 and the balance amounts payable to them as per the agreement dated February 23, 1989 be forfeited.
>
> With regards to Sanjay Manjrekar, M. Venkatramana, Sanjeev Sharma, Ajay Sharma, N. Hirwani and Robin Singh, the disciplinary committee came to the unanimous conclusion that considering that it was their first tour of official Test matches and the players not being experienced enough to understand the implications of breach of discipline, they be directed to pay a penalty of 15,000 rupees each on or before 14 September 1989 and in default of such payment be debarred from playing in matches under the auspices of the BCCI until payment is made. Furthermore, the balance amount of fees payable to the six players as per the agreement stands forfeited.
>
> With regard to Chetan Sharma and Arshad Ayub, they have been given a further opportunity to appear before the disciplinary committee on September 15 at the Wankhede Stadium in Bombay.... The disciplinary committee at its meeting on July 1 considered the replies given by the cricketers except Chetan Sharma and Arshad Ayub and came to the unanimous conclusion that prima facie the explanations given by them were not satisfactory and accordingly requested them to appear for producing witness and evidence if they so wanted.[3]

Such stern action against the players was prompted by a complaint lodged by the national cricket boards of the US and Canada with the ICC.[4] Following this, the banned cricketers, shocked by the Board's decision, declared in a statement that a ban

> had never been imposed except for participation in matches organized by Kerry Packer or for playing in South Africa, or on account of conviction in drug related offences. In India even a cricketer against whom murder charges were pending has been rightly permitted to play. Playing of exhibition matches for the promotion of cricket cannot be considered identical to playing in South Africa.[5]

They concluded saying, 'We want to play for the country but with dignity and honour. We have fared badly in the West Indies but we do not feel we ought to be punished for that.'[6]

The ban, the *Telegraph* argued, was a telling blow to player power:

> The BCCI has struck a savage blow to player power. It has, at least for the moment, made it abundantly clear who is the boss. The message to the players is quite simple: the BCCI is going not only to call the shots, but play them too.... The disciplinary committee was set up in May, held sittings in June and July and decided on action only today.... The working committee meeting in Bangalore where the players' violation of the Code of Conduct was first discussed, had seen a rare unanimity in that everyone wanted the players to be put in their place. In this chapter of the board versus the players row the board was on a better wicket. Memories of skirmishes over players writing during international fixtures and differences in sporting of logos were all too recent.... The players, who undertook the North American trip, clearly did not anticipate severe action for disregarding a Presidential directive. With generous help from Sunil Gavaskar, Dilip Vengsarkar and Kapil Dev chalked up the players' strategy. The reply to the show cause would be common. Under the circumstances there could not have been a better move. But the Board had better ideas....
>
> Interestingly, the one year ban comes soon after Dr. Ali Bacher has signed up rebel Englishmen for two tours of South Africa. There have been reports that Dr. Bacher's men have approached cricketers from the subcontinent. And it will not be surprising if Dr. Bacher's London based agents arrive here for a talk with the six Indians.
>
> Indian cricket will obviously never be the same again but as former cricketer Nari Contractor explained, 'a line had to be drawn somewhere.'[7]

The players soon gained a footing, when a Supreme Court bench headed by Justice Venkataramiah ordered the BCCI to arrive at a settlement with them. Venkataramiah's decree that any further litigation could adversely affect the Board and might have disturbing implications forced the Board to lift the ban in an Extraordinary Working Committee meeting on 15 September 1989.

Commenting on the BCCI's decision to revoke the ban, the *Telegraph* declared:

> The Board of Control for cricket in India today unconditionally lifted the one year ban as well as waived the fines imposed on six top cricketers for violating the West Indies tour contract after they made a fresh appeal to the Board.
>
> A special working committee meeting of the BCCI, which considered the cricketers' fresh appeal felt that 'there was sincerity in the players appeal' submitted today. It therefore decided to take a 'lenient view' and lift the 38 day old ban.

The committee not only pardoned the breach of contract but also waived the 35,000 and 50,000 rupees fines imposed on the banned cricketers and six others respectively for playing matches in the United States and Canada, defying the BCCI President's directive to return home from the West Indies tour.

Another beneficiary of today's meeting was Mohinder Amarnath who had been fined 20,000 rupees for calling national selectors a 'bunch of jokers'. The committee decided to drop the fine in this case also. Five of the six banned cricketers...were called today to present their case together for the last time while Mohinder Amarnath was heard separately. The sixth banned player, Ravi Shastri, is in England.[8]

Denying that the BCCI was under pressure to lift the ban or that there was any loss of prestige in granting concessions to the players, the Working Committee issued the following statement:

This is about the appeal on behalf of the six players...against the order of the disciplinary committee debarring them for a period of one year...from playing cricket matches conducted and/or authorized by the BCCI in India or through its affiliated associations.... The proceedings before the disciplinary committee emanated for the breach of clause 3(s) read with clause 7 of the aforesaid agreements dated February 23 and 28 1989.

The aforesaid five players on their behalf and on behalf of Ravi Shastri tendered the following statement to the Appellate Committee:

It has never been the intention of any player to confront the authority of the Board in any way. In view of that and all the surrounding facts and circumstances of the case, we would like to re-iterate that there was never any intention to disregard the directives of the Board President. Therefore, in the larger interest of the game, and with a view to preserve the healthy and co-operative relations with the Board and the players we regret the controversy generated so that the matter may be closed and we can get on with the game of cricket.

The Appellate Committee went through the record and proceedings of the DC and heard the aggrieved players. Having heard the players and having considered the written statement filed by them [it] feels there is sincerity in the statement made by them.... It feels that a lenient view of the matter needs to be taken in view of the facts and circumstances stated above. The Committee is of the unanimous opinion that the penalty of ban as well as the forfeiture of the amount needs to be vacated with a warning to the concerned players not to repeat such acts in future and that they would endeavour to maintain the high standard of discipline.... The Committee further felt that the cases of the players who have not formally appealed being of a similar nature have to be dealt with in the same way and the committee suo moto decided that the fine imposed on them is hereby waived.[9]

Following the announcements by the BCCI Working Committee, Mohinder Amarnath, who had elaborated in his syndicated news columns why he had called the national selectors a 'bunch of jokers' in November 1988 changed his stance and declared that, 'the expression was never intended to hurt the selectors but was an instant outburst of his feelings at being unfairly treated. He regretted the use of it if it had "affected the sensibilities of the selectors".'[10]

All cricketers, past and contemporary, welcomed the truce, expressing satisfaction that the controversy had come to an end. Lala Amarnath summed up the mood stating:

I am very happy that the ban has been lifted. The ban and the fine, in my opinion, were going to damage cricket as well as the prestige of the country. I hope the cricketers and the august body, BCCI, will have a more cordial relationship. Let bygones be bygones. God bless Indian cricket.[11]

Epilogue

In a book on controversies that have plagued Indian cricket, it is impossible to talk about all those individuals who have affected and shaped the fortunes of the game. If delved into, many of these would emerge as equally significant episodes in the history of the game as the ones discussed in detail in this book. The historian is, however, constrained by the fragmented nature of source material, which leaves several gaps unfilled. In the course of my research, I came across fascinating episodes, which (regrettably), could not be built into a coherent narrative in the manner that episodes have been reconstructed in this volume. Many of these were indeed as exciting and controversial but they were fragments which I was unable to flesh out and situate in the broader history of the game, purely on account of non-availability of records. However, these fragments stir the imagination and it would be unfair not to even mention them in this volume. In this section, I will make note of some of these fragments, strands from a lost history of the game.

Historians of cricket in India often wonder why there is little in terms of written records from which a history of Indian cricket may be reconstructed. Compared with the volumes written on English cricket history, histories of the game in India are rare and piecemeal. A possible answer is that record keeping has been one of the most neglected areas of Indian cricket, evident from the limited number of monographs that exist on the history of the game in India. Why there is so little documentation may be better understood perhaps from the following incident described by Shapoorjee Sorabjee in his '*A Chronicle of Cricket among Parsees and The Struggle: Polo versus Cricket*' (1897). He speaks of the annual general meeting of the Elphinstone Cricket Club, one of the best-known cricket clubs of the time. During the meeting, the Secretary, Mr. Dhanjibhoy S. Divecha was asked to present his report on the functioning of the Club. To everyone's surprise he stated, 'Brothers, I wrote the report on the wall of my house for the sake of permanency, but unfortunately my father got it white washed and the report along with it.'[1] The committee found this explanation unsatisfactory and Mr. Divecha was eventually removed from his post.

While the paucity of written records serves as a serious impediment, selective use of source material by commentators and scholars has also obscured realities, as well as unpleasant memories which are no less significant. That communal hatred in Indian cricket was commented upon in British newspapers is little known. This rare occurrence took place on 16 February 1936 when the *Star* reported that, 'Hindu Muslim hatred may ruin England tour'. It went on to suggest that:

> For years there has been the utmost difficulty in choosing any Indian side. Muslims insist that players of their religion should predominate. Hindus believe that none but men of their faith ought to play. Form has been the last thing considered. Now the religious war, just as fierce as the bodyline outburst has flared up with greater intensity. The chances are that the team to represent India here will not be the strongest that could have been sent.[2]

Though there were protests from the BCCI soon after, the *Star*'s words proved true. Vizzy's team fared poorly in England in a tour dominated by off-the-field controversies, the unceremonious sacking of Lala Amarnath being the highlight.

The selective reportage of unpleasant episodes has also overlooked hardships faced by many of the nation's leading cricketers in the 1930s and 1940s. With modern Indian cricketers being the richest sportspersons of the country, it is difficult to understand the fate of our veteran cricket stars from half-a-century ago. D.D. Hindlekar, one of India's most talented wicketkeepers, died prematurely at a very young age for want of proper treatment in 1948. Hindlekar was superb behind the stumps during India's tour of England in 1936. Even after his death, the BCCI, cash-strapped since inception, was not in a position to help his relatives. After repeated appeals by his wife, a cabaret dance performance was organised in Bombay to help the suffering family. A purse of Rs. 7,000 was raised from the cabaret, which was handed over to Mrs. Hindlekar. Another grand player, Amir Elahi, one of the nation's leading spinners of the 1930s had to trade his art in local matches for a rupee each for survival.

Even commentary, which is the most lucrative source of employment for retired cricketers in recent times, was hardly a well-developed art till the 1950s and 1960s. Broadcasters now have teams of seven or eight commentators commenting on a Test match. In India, through the 1930s and 1940s, Bobby Talyarkhan was the lone commentator speaking for over six hours a day. He began his tryst with commentary in the Parsees versus Mohammedans match at the Bombay Gymkhana in 1934, which was the first match to be broadcast live by All India Radio. From this year onwards, he single-handedly broadcast ball-by-ball commentary on all the matches of the Bombay Pentangular and Ranji Trophy tournaments for over a decade-and-a-half. His longest broadcast was the Bombay–Poona Ranji Trophy match at Poona, which went into the sixth day. Despite his contributions to the promotion of Indian cricket (he was also instrumental in starting a sports page in Indian newspapers), Bobby Talyarkhan was unceremoniously dumped by the Board of Control for Cricket in India and All India Radio in 1949–50. His own attitude, however, did have a role to play in his exit. Talyarkhan was unwilling to share the commentary box with others and was eventually forced to move to Ceylon to practise his art.

Finally, it will be of interest to note that cricket in post-independence India, unlike its colonial counterpart, had become a monopoly of the affluent élite. An escalation, from the early 1950s, in the cost of tickets and the guarantee money to be paid by a centre hosting an international encounter was responsible for this development, among many other factors. The sudden rise in the cost of tickets provoked widespread outrage among ordinary people, who, reports indicate, were unable to buy tickets. It was recollected that in the days of the Pentangular, all small clubs having practice nets on the maidan were issued tickets for their members at subsidised rates, and a modest sum was charged for admission to the grand stand for the public. Twelve days of the Pentangular could be enjoyed with all the ancillary facilities of transport and refreshments for a payment of Rs. 10 per head. Even for the Gymkhana stands, the price of a season ticket was not more than Rs. 10 per person.

Following this escalation, the Bombay Cricket Association was expected to pay the Board Rs. 30,000 as guarantee money and Rs. 40,000 from ticket sales (at the rate of Rs. 4 per ticket), causing them to price tickets at amounts beyond the reach of the ordinary enthusiast. They were also expected to pay Indian players Rs. 250 per head as match fee and bear the expenses of hosting rival teams. The situation produced the following comment in the *Free Press Journal*:

> The stage is definitely reached when it would be advisable to consider whether it is worthwhile to have a foreign side playing in Bombay, which costs the city not less than 100,000 actual expenditure. If only 10 per cent

of the total expenditure were to be utilized for providing sporting facilities to students, we would probably get much more results.[3]

That the price hike provoked considerable outrage is evident from a series of letters published in the *Free Press Journal*:

Enhanced Rates: I read your comment re: the entrance rate for the big cricket matches, I too join in drawing the attention of the authorities. As you state, I realize CCI needs more money to meet the expenses of bringing up cricket, I quite appreciate your contention and that of the CCI, but I find no reason to raise the rate since during the last cricket matches, with rates lower than the present, they were able to assess a lakh and few thousands as net profit. The crowds during the recent matches were diminished by 30 to 35 per cent when compared to the matches versus the West Indies and the Commonwealth XI; whereas it would have been a full house. If this rate, as you state, is fixed by the CCI after 'full consideration', I should say that they have lost sight of the economics of 'little purse' as well as defeating the very purpose, namely, making the common people cricket minded. In whose welcome participation lies the success of cricket, football and sports in India? Don't you think that as the rate stands today, only one man will enter grudgingly where three more would have ungrudgingly done, had the rates been brought down?[4]

In complete disregard of such discontent, the BCCI, in its efforts to facilitate the MCC's visit to India in 1951–52, opted to shelve the Schools Cricket Championship for two years at the first instance. The argument put forth was that the championship was doing no good:

The schools cricket tournament 'is doing no good', according to Mr. A.S. De Mello, President of the board, who is sponsoring the move to abandon the championship for two years in the first instance. Lack of interest among schools authorities, it is learnt, caused great difficulties in completing the early rounds, and last year the semi finals were not played.[5]

The Board also desired to temporarily shelve the Ranji Trophy tournament. Such proposals provoked anxiety among cricket enthusiasts in all parts of the country. Commenting on them the *Times of India* reported:

Nothing could be more harmful to the interests of cricket in India than the move to replace the Ranji trophy competition with a zonal tournament. Ostensibly this change is intended to meet the exigencies of the forthcoming MCC tour. But it is by now painfully evident that the real intent behind the proposal is to establish a precedent for all future visits of foreign teams. The glamour of sponsoring tours at home and abroad appears to have overcome the highly susceptible pundits of the Board of Control for Cricket in India. These foreign carnivals may mean more gate money though, considering the outlay and disbursements involved both at home and abroad, many will question even this. What Indian cricket needs is not glamourisation but consolidation and the Board of control's lack of interest in the constructive side of the game was represented by the Schools' Championship of India, the Inter University Championship and the Cricket championship. It is a few years since the cricket board unburdened itself of the second of these tournaments and it now proposes to abandon the competition for schools and to bypass the national tournament. Genuine lovers of the game will strongly resist a move which, whatever its motivations, can only result in Indian cricket, bereft of its nurseries and training grounds, being wiped off the test map.[6]

The report concluded by declaring that the decision on the national championship would indicate whether the BCCI was committed to a policy of fostering the game in the country or whether it preferred to sponsor *tamasha*s.

The steep rise in the cost of tickets, contemporary newspaper reports noted, transformed the composition of the cricket crowd, making the stadium a preserve of the affluent. The disappearance of the common man from the grounds left many noted commentators of the time disillusioned. Bobby Talyarkhan argued in the *Free Press Journal*:

Candidly, our present crowds give me a pain in the neck. Not one in ten comes to the cricket for the game, and only one in ten knows anything about its finer points. I hear it is the same all over the country these days, as it is in Bombay, the cricket crowd being composed largely of noisy, oily tamasha mad people, one or two names of stars on their lips, understanding that one team is leading the other in the score books. Fat and greasy nouveauriche men, with fat and greasy spouses and fat and greasy brats turning the stands into a common bazar, a mohalla, anything but a refined cricket arena. Children are dragged along to our big cricket, youngsters who should be trying to do a bit of sweating themselves, dragged with their autograph books and their cameras, utterly unschooled in anything to do with cricket, trying to ape their elders in making just a holiday, a five days outing which they never belonged to and never will. Am I nasty? I intend to be; if the turnstiles of Indian cricket are going to click to these people, we might as well write off the game now and rest content with nostalgic memories of when cricket was a pastime out of the topmost drawer.[7]

The situation came to a head when the government decided to reduce its annual sports grant to schools in western India. The grant had been used to promote cricket in these institutions. The decision resulted in a cut in the cricket budget of high schools by over 50 per cent, and forced authorities to run one team only, instead of dividing the boys into senior and junior sides, as had been the practice earlier.

D.B. Deodhar summed up the uncertain situation by declaring that after the decline of princely patronage, Indian cricket had ceased to appeal to the fancy of its former admirers. Cricket, he opined, would have to struggle hard in post-independence India to keep its head up and prove its utility to the policy makers if it were to enjoy patronage. With independence the greatest props of the sport had disappeared:

> It is therefore to be seen how the new Indian governors and high ranking officials look at it and how they encourage it directly or otherwise. The prospects however are not bright in the present days of stress and strain when the leaders who hold the destiny of the land in their hands have hardly any time to think of sports, even supposing that they had the will for it. Anyway, the former recognition for this game and the consequent glamour are gone and with them the attraction for it with the young generation.[8]

Deodhar commented that the game, which had earlier been sustained by a steady supply of young talent, generated by the well-developed structure of school cricket, was gradually drying up. The schools in the Bombay Presidency no longer had government grants for the upkeep of the game, forcing the closure of nets in most institutions. The BCCI, too, did nothing to induce these schools to have a net reserved for cricket:

> For many years past, some of the Indian princes had been patronizing cricket and cricketers maintaining their state teams. Some were vying with one another to engage the top class cricketers to win the Ranji trophy for their Elevens. Now things have completely changed and the maharajas are anxious for their own existence. It is thus doubtful if they can maintain their teams in future. The disbanded players will have a hard lot if they have not developed any other qualification except their game. In the absence of regular professionalism in our country, these star cricketers would be forced to seek other avocations for their living. Their game as a result is bound to suffer. The disappearance of princely patrons may be a blessing in the politics of democratic India, but it will be a blow to costly games like cricket, unless the people come forward to patronize it.[9]

The schools and colleges that retained infrastructure and training facilities were the premier institutions, mostly attended by boys and girls from affluent families. It is only in recent times, after the boom in sponsorship, that the BCCI has undertaken measures to redress this problem, converting Indian cricket into a meritocracy.

Concluding Remarks

In modern India, no hyperbole is sufficient to capture the importance of cricket in the country's national life. This is because India, the most populous nation in the world, is a rather insignificant presence globally once we account for the export of software professionals to West Asia and the West. This marginality is especially prominent in sports. In the Sydney Olympics of 2000 India won a solitary bronze medal. The country continues to baffle with the panoply of anomalies it produces. Consider the fact that 44 per cent of Indians still spend less than a dollar a day, 70 of a 1,000 Indian children die before their first birthday and another 25 die before they turn five. In world politics, India remains a distant presence—her pleas against terrorist violence fall on deaf ears, communal conflict continues to be a looming spectre and over a third of the population lives on the streets. 'Brain drain' remains one of the biggest threats that confront the nation.

However, when we turn our attention to a very particular arena of Indian sport, cricket, this narrative of 'backwardness', 'catching up' and 'gloom' begins to falter. Cricket is the only realm where Indians can flex their muscles on the world stage; it is the nation's only instrument with which to have a crack at world domination. It is, to put it simply, much more than a 'game' for Indians. Such an intense engagement with this wonderful game began more than a century ago, and if anything, it promises to become even more energetic over the coming decades, giving rise in turn to more controversies, creating in effect an even greater furore.

Notes

Series Editor's Foreword

1. John Keats, 'On First Looking into Chapman's Homer' in Francis T. Palgrave, *The Golden Treasury* (London: Macmillan,1955), p. 199.
2. Boria Majumdar, *Lost Histories of Indian Cricket: Battles off the Pitch* (London: Routledge, 2005), p. 107.

1. Empire vs. Parsee XI

1. For details see, Richard Cashman, *Patrons, Players and the Crowd* (Calcutta: Orient Longman, 1979), p. 28.
2. For details see, Mihir Bose, *History of Indian Cricket* (London: Andre Deutsch, 2002), p. 22; Ramachandra Guha, 'Searching for Space', in *A Corner of a Foreign Field* (London: Picador, 2002).
3. Guha, *A Corner of a Foreign Field*, p. 20.
4. The captain of the Parsee touring team in London in 1888 also voiced the grievance of the Parsee cricketers of Bombay. In an interview with a correspondent of the *Birmingham Daily Times*, P.D. Kanga declared, 'They are handicapped in other ways than in the restricted time for play owing to the fierce rays of a torrid sun: polo is played on their wickets, and the turf is too scorched and dry for true bowling and safe batting.'
5. For details see, Shapoorjee Sorabjee, *A Chronicle of Cricket among Parsees and The Struggle: Polo versus Cricket* (Bombay, published by the author, 1897); Quoted in Guha, *A Corner of a Foreign Field*.
6. The resolution passed by the public works department on 17 April 1882 declared:

    Messrs Shapoorjee Sorabjee and other inhabitants of Bombay are informed in reply to their petition dated 27 March 1882, to the address of his Excellency the Governor in Council, that instructions will be issued to permit the native cricketers to use the Esplanade Parade ground, when not required by Government for military and other purposes.

7. On 9 February 1883, Shapoorjee Sorabjee and others addressed another petition to Sir James Fergusson, Governor of Bombay. This petition asserted:

> With reference to the Government Resolution No 105 R of 1882, Public Works Department, dated 17 April 1882, with regard to the use of the Esplanade Parade Ground, we beg to bring to the notice of your Excellency in Council for your kind consideration that the cricketers have almost not enjoyed the benefit of that resolution, and they are now as badly off as they had been before. The ground is still used for Polo to the disadvantage of cricket players.

They attached a list of 12 days when polo was played on the ground since the passing of the resolution. The petition concluded saying:

> We, therefore, on behalf of the cricketers, humbly pray to your Excellency to direct that proper effect be given to the above referred resolution of 17 April 1882, so that polo may not be played on the ground in question, and the plot of cricket ground kept enclosed by the Gymkhana may be open for cricketers.

Responding to their petition, W.A. Baker, Under Secretary to the government wrote:

> Messrs Shapoorjee Sorabjee and Manekdas Ramdas Dalal are informed with reference to their petition dated 9 February 1883, to the address of His Excellency the Governor in Council, that it is not in accordance with the facts of the case to state that 'they are now as badly off as they had been before'. By their own shewing polo has been played 12 days in about 10 months instead of twice a week as heretofore. They are further informed that it was never intended to deprive the cricketers of the Gymkhana of the reserved ground they at present occupy without occasion and due notice and that their respect in this respect cannot be acceded to.

Subsequently, Mr. Cecil Gray, Polo Secretary of the Gymkhana submitted a petition to the Government on 30 May 1883:

> bringing to the notice of HE the Governor in Council the fact that in addition to those who actually engage in the game of Polo, there is a large number of persons who, as spectators, take the greatest interest and derive the greatest enjoyment from the game; and praying that, as the only open space of sufficient size and in other respects suitable for polo is the Parade ground, His Excellency in Council will be pleased to cancel the Government Resolution No. 139E. 620, dated 13 April 1882, which prohibits polo on the parade ground, and again permit that game to be

> played on the ground referred to, on two evenings of the week, in the same way as it had been for many years previous to the passing of the Resolution above quoted.

In response, the government passed the following resolution:

> In modification of the orders contained in Government Resolution No. 139E. 620 dated 13 April 1882, Government are now pleased to rule that the Esplanade Parade ground may be used for Polo on one evening of the week and also in the morning of the Brigade Holiday.

This controversy dragged on through the 1880s and a number of letters, for and against, were published by both parties in the pages of the *Times of India*. As an outcome of this controversy, Lord Harris, upon his arrival in Bombay as Governor in 1890, allotted land to the Gymkhanas of the three communities, Hindu, Muslim and Parsee, placing them on equal terms with each other. They were to pay a token rent of Rs. 12 on the land.

8. Guha, 'Searching for Space', in *A Corner of a Foreign Field*, p. 28.
9. Shapoorjee Sorabjee, *A Chronicle of Cricket among Parsees*, p. 18.
10. Ibid.
11. Ibid., p. 19.
12. Ibid., pp. 19–20.
13. Ibid., pp. 20–21.
14. Ibid., p. 22.
15. *Times of India* (15 April 1931).
16. Ibid. (16 April 1931).
17. Ibid. (20 April 1931).
18. Ibid. (18 April 1931).
19. Ibid. (16 May 1931).
20. Ibid.
21. Ibid.
22. Ibid. (18 May 1931).
23. Ibid. (8 June 1931).
24. Ibid. (15 June 1931).
25. Ibid. (4 July 1931).
26. Ibid. (21 July 1931).

2. The Cricketing Jam

1. Satadru Sen, 'Chameleon Games: Ranjitsinhji's Politics of Race and Gender', in *Journal of Colonialism and Colonial History*, 2:3 (2001).
2. Charles Kincaid, *The Land of Ranji and Duleep* (London: Blackwood and Sons, 1931), p. 105. Also see, Simon Wilde, *Ranji—A Genius Rich and Strange* (London: Kingswood Press, 1990), pp. 9–24.
3. Kincaid, *The Land of Ranji and Duleep*, p. 105.

4. Ibid., p. 106. Umedsinhji had been poisoned by members of Jam Vibhaji's zenana. Kincaid describes the incident thus:

> No greater calamity could have befallen the unhappy boy than his adoption. Terrible as are the tempers of the Olympian Immortals, they pale before the furies of an Indian zenana. Dhanbai, maddened by the failure of Kalobha's murderous plot and the exclusion of her only son, took steps to ensure that the new heir, at least, should not enjoy his good fortune. A dose of arsenic in Raysinhji's (Umedsinhji was christened Raysinhji after his adoption) evening meal, a few hours of mortal agony, and the gallant young Jadeja prince lay dead in the royal palace.

5. Wilde, *Ranji—A Genius Rich and Strange*, pp. 16–19.
6. Ibid.
7. Kincaid, *The Land of Ranji and Duleep*, pp. 111–12.
8. Ibid.
9. Ibid., p. 113.
10. Ibid., p. 114.
11. Ibid., p. 112.
12. Ibid.
13. Wilde, *Ranji—A Genius Rich and Strange*, p. 98.
14. Ibid., p. 99.
15. Ranji toured Bengal in 1898–99 as part of the Maharaja of Patiala's team. During this tour, the Calcutta Town Hall organised a function to felicitate him, spending Rs. 3,000, a huge sum by contemporary standards; For details of this tour see, Saradaranjan Ray, 'Cricket Khela' in *Mukul* (1899).
16. Wilde, *Ranji—A Genius Rich and Strange*, p. 99.
17. Simon Wilde, p. 226. Sen in his work on Ranji 'Chameleon Games' fails to take into account these facts and goes on to say that:

> In 1898, he travelled to India and stayed for a year. He petitioned the colonial government—and George Hamilton, the Secretary of State for India—to intervene on his behalf in the politics of Nawanagar. Hamilton curtly refused. Ranjitsinhji would learn that the colonial political establishment was not particularly impressed by his credentials as a cricketer and a celebrity. Whereas the British at home might appreciate the novelty of an Indian who behaved, dressed and played as if he were English, the same transgressions were fundamentally threatening to the British who were directly in charge of running the colonial administration. They understood very well that Englishness gave Indians like Ranjitsinhji the license to make political demands, and they were unwilling to make any concessions.

18. Wilde, *Ranji—A Genius Rich and Strange*, p. 108.
19. Ibid., pp. 108–09.
20. Roland Wild, *The Biography of His Highness Shri Sir Ranjitsinhji* (London: Rich and Cowan, 1934), pp. 16–18; Quoted in Sen, 'Chameleon Games'.
21. Wilde, *Ranji—A Genius Rich and Strange*, pp. 93–94.

22. Ibid. Also see Government of Bombay, Political Department file 1843A, OIOC (1909). It is worth noting as Satadru Sen has argued that Kachar would himself be investigated by the colonial government in 1912 and was accused of theft and forgery. Bombay Political Department file 2028A OIOC (1912).
23. Boria Majumdar, 'Ranji—His Love, Life and Letters', *Oulook* (2 June 2002).
24. Wilde, *Ranji—A Genius Rich and Strange*, p. 166.
25. Ibid., pp. 168–70.
26. Ibid., p. 170.
27. Ibid.
28. Death of Jassaji and Claims, OIOC (R/2/676/20), Petition submitted by Lakhuba to the Political Agent of Rajkot.
29. Ibid.
30. Memorial submitted by Lakhuba to the Governor and President in Council, Bombay, on the subject of his right to succession to the Nawanagar Gadi, OIOC (R/2/676/20).
31. Ibid.
32. Ibid.
33. Ibid.
34. Wilde, *Ranji—A Genius Rich and Strange*, p. 172.
35. He returned to play for Sussex in 1920 at the age of 47. Wilde (*Ranji—A Genius Rich and Strange*, p. 226) describes the game thus:

> Overweight and certainly no longer lithe, he went in at number eight, batted fifty minutes on a good pitch and not without skill gathered 16 runs, but all his reactions were sluggish and he had to keep looking to play the ball away on the leg side, the side of his good eye. Later, in the field, he had further difficulty in focussing on the ball and when not at slip had to scheme to save himself exertion.

He had played two more games before he was injured.
36. Bose, *History of Indian Cricket*, p. 43.
37. For details of this view see, A.S. De Mello, *Portrait of Indian Sport* (London: Pan Macmillan, 1960).
38. Wilde, *Ranji—A Genius Rich and Strange*, pp. 240–41.
39. Ibid. Also see, Kincaid, *The Land of Ranji and Duleep*, p. 125.
40. Wilde, *Ranji—A Genius Rich and Strange*, p. 241.
41. Ibid., p. 234.
42. Ibid., p. 240. Even after the First World War, Ranji, as Satadru Sen ('Chameleon Games', http://muse.jhu.edu/journals/journal_of_colonial-ism_and_colonial_history/v002/2.3sen.html) has shown, was critical of the English:

> When the Great War broke out, Ranjitsinhji was quick to volunteer. He spent the winter of 1914–1915 in the rear trenches of France: complaining about the cold, the dampness and the dirt, but safe. To his great

excitement, his commanding officer (General Cookson, 'who has been a brick to me') allowed him to venture briefly within range of the enemy guns, but pulled him back before he could come to any harm. Ranjitsinhji was in fact wounded in the course of this overseas adventure, but it was in a hunting accident in England, during a break from the miseries of Europe. Nevertheless, his very presence in the vicinity of the fighting allowed him to claim, 'I was the only chief to take an active part.'

The immediate results of this display of military commitment were mixed. Ranjitsinhji received a fifteen-gun salute, and the ranks of Maharaja and Lieutenant-Colonel. He accepted the new honours with less than perfect grace. He had hoped that the military services of the princes would be rewarded by the grant of territory. When this hope came to nothing, he commented, acidly and incorrectly, that he did not need the British to make him a Maharaja, as 'this has been my hereditary title all my life'.

43. Cashman, *Patrons, Players and the Crowd*, pp. 36–37.
44. Kincaid, *The Land of Ranji and Duleep*, pp. 137–38.

3. Birthpangs

1. The Maharajas of Patiala, who had taken to cricket patronage in the late nineteenth century, looked upon cricket to assert equality with the colonial masters. They had their own cricket grounds at Patiala and Chail. Maharaja Rajendra Singh initiated cricket patronage at Patiala employing cricketers from across the country. Under him and his successors, Patiala gave India a number of its leading cricketers, players who dominated Indian cricket in the years 1890–1940.

No ruler, it has been argued, had recruited cricketers on the scale begun by the Maharaja of Patiala since 1895. Merit, it is evident from the list of the players, was the primary consideration, deemed more important than considerations of caste, creed or economic background. Maharaja Bhupinder Singh, son of Rajendra Singh, continued this tradition of patronage after his father's premature death at the age of 28. However, under him the reason for patronage had changed. It was more to outdo his rival, the Maharajkumar of Vizianagram, that Bhupinder Singh extended patronage to great Indian cricketers like Lala Amarnath, Anwar Hussain, Lall Singh, Nazir and Wazir Ali. They were patronised by the Patiala Darbar, which absorbed 'any sportsman who had made a name for himself at cricket, wrestling, athletics or some other sport, into the state service'. While some sportsmen, such as Colonel Mistry, were entrusted positions of responsibility at Patiala, most were not and were left free to pursue careers in sport. In recognition of his patronage, Maharaja Bhupinder Singh was appointed President of the Cricket Club of India in 1937. He was also nominated President of the Indian Olympic Association (IOA) in 1939 and held this position till 1960 when his younger brother Raja Bhalindra Singh succeeded him.

2. Established in December 1928, the Board is celebrating its 75th anniversary in 2003–04.

3. Set up in 1933, the Cricket Club of India played a pivotal role in the development of cricket in late colonial India.

4. It remains unaccounted how Vizzy managed to get Hobbes and Sutcliffe to agree. Hobbes had earlier refused all offers of playing in India. In the course of their visit they even played for the Sporting Union, a local club side in Calcutta. For details on this match, see, Boria Majumdar, 'Believe it or Not', in the *Times of India*, Kolkata (19 January 2002).

5. With a team that included the best of national and international talent, Vizzy's team won 17 out of the 18 matches played in the tour.

6. For details see, Boria Majumdar, 'Palace Intrigue', in *Wisden Asia Cricket* (September 2002).

7. *Times of India* (3 September 1931).

8. Ibid. (10 September 1931).

9. Ibid.

10. Ibid. (14 September 1931).

11. Ibid. In another report titled 'Cricket tour: MCC arrangements Progressing', the *Times of India* of 12 October 1931 reported that:

> it will be recalled that early last month doubts were expressed owing to the financial stringency and political uncertainty the required funds from the provincial associations might not be forthcoming. The princely decision of the Maharajkumar of Vizianagram of Rs. 50,000 encouraged the Board to cable the MCC ensuring them of the strongest representative team visiting England next year.

12. *Times of India* (28 November 1931).

13. Reporting this move the *Times of India* of 11 December 1931 declared:

> His Highness the Maharaja of Patiala has consented to stage two trial matches at Patiala from 23 January to 29 January 1932.... A very urgent meeting of the full selection committee will be held on December 15 when several important matters in regard to the selection of the team to visit England in 1932 will be considered.... The meeting will draw up teams for the trial matches at Patiala.

14. The Board faced acute financial crisis till the middle of the 1940s. In 1936 the crisis had become so acute that the Ranji Trophy, the national championship started in 1934 under the aegis of the Board, was about to be stopped. It was eventually played with the Bombay Pentangular committee paying the necessary expenses.

15. Mihir Bose, *History of Indian Cricket* (London: Andre Deutsch, 2002), p. 68.

16. *Times of India* (16 January 1932).

17. Ibid. (20 January 1932).

18. This was evident when R.E. Grant-Govan declared during the tea interval on the final day of the first trial:

> We have now come to the concluding stage of the first trial here to select the team to go to England and I feel that before we break up, on behalf of the cricketers and the Board of Control, I would like to thank Your Highness for your hospitality and convey our deep sense of gratitude for all the help that you have given for the future of Indian cricket.

For details see, *Times of India* (27 January 1932).
19. *Times of India* (4 February 1932).
20. Ibid. (6 February 1932).
21. Ibid.
22. Ibid. *The Morning Post*, in welcoming the visit of the Indian cricketers, paid a tribute to the Maharaja of Patiala as captain saying that 'he could be relied upon to get the most and the best out of his team'.
23. Ibid. Another report published on 14 February stated:

> The captaincy, on the whole, has been put into good hands. The Maharaja of Patiala certainly knows a lot about the game, and if, perhaps, his fielding will leave a lot to be desired, it is not expected that he will play in all the matches.

24. Ibid. (16 February 1932).
25. Ibid. He concluded his statement saying:

> I expect to be visiting Europe very shortly for my health and shall also be spending some time in England when I shall be at Lords to watch India make her debut in her first Test match and when in England I shall be happy to render any advice to the Board and to the team if called upon to do so. Wishing the tour to England an unqualified success and knowing the entire team as I do, I have every hope that they will play the game and be the true ambassadors of India on the cricket field and away from it.

26. Ibid. (3 March 1932).
27. Ibid.
28. Ibid. (24 March 1932).
29. The Maharaja of Porbander played in the first four matches of the tour averaging 0.66 runs per inning.
30. Descriptions of the tour in the *Times of India* make it clear that internal dissensions among the players had adversely affected the performances of the team. For detailed descriptions on how the players had been alienated from Nayudu, see, Bose, *History of Indian Cricket,* pp. 78–79.
31. The building of the Feroz Shah Kotla stadium in Delhi was due largely to the donation of Rs. 500,000 by the Maharaja of Bhavnagar.
32. Bose, *History of Indian Cricket,* p. 80.
33. Ibid., pp. 78–79.

34. Ibid., p. 83.
35. For details see, Majumdar, 'Palace Intrigue'.
36. Quoted in Majumdar, 'Palace Intrigue'.
37. Ibid.
38. Ibid.
39. This tournament was patronised by the Nizam of Hyderabad. It is still played and is looked upon as an arena where young cricketers can make their mark and impress the national selectors.
40. Bose, *History of Indian Cricket*, p. 93.
41. Quoted in Majumdar, 'Palace Intrigue'.
42. Bombay has won the Ranji trophy more than any other team in the country, bearing out the contention that from the 1930s it had established itself as the home of Indian cricket.

4. The Amarnath Affair

1. *Times of India* (22 June 1936).
2. Bose, *History of Indian Cricket*, 2002, p. 100.
3. *Times of India* (16 February 1936).
4. Ibid. (21 July 1936). The entire affair was reported in detail on this day.
5. Ibid.
6. Ibid.
7. Ibid. Amarnath told his captain all of them were friends and that he did not expect the captain to be unreasonably curt or rude because he was doing his best for the team. He also stated that the captain could not insult the players because they were not professionals but amateurs and were not paid to play cricket.
8. Ibid.
9. Ibid.
10. Ibid.
11. Ibid.
12. Ibid.
13. It is interesting to note that Elahi, under severe financial strain, used to bowl in exhibition matches for Re. 1 to sustain himself while D.D. Hindlekar, India's wicketkeeper in the 1936 tour, died prematurely without treatment in a state of abject poverty.
14. In this tour Baqa Jilani earned his maiden Test cap by abusing C.K. Nayudu at the breakfast table under instructions from Vizzy.
15. *Times of India* (21 July 1936).
16. Ibid.
17. Ibid.
18. Ibid.
19. Ibid.
20. Ibid.

21. Ibid. (20 June 1936). He also stated that he intended to see the Nawab of Bhopal soon after his arrival in India and place the facts before him. 'I felt so upset after the happenings that I cried nearly all night.' Another report filed from London on the same day asserted, 'The members of the All India cricket team and Indian cricket enthusiasts here deprecate the action of sending Amarnath home and express the opinion that the differences could have been smoothened over without such drastic action.' Another news story titled 'Previous Lapse' declared:

> There is no doubt that the playing strength of the Indian team will be weakened by the absence of Amarnath. He has been the team's chief run getter, having three centuries to his credit, and having set up a record for an Indian batsman by hitting two centuries in the same match. Against Essex he scored 130 and 107. His dismissal for what amounts to insubordination recalls the incident in September 1934, when he refused to play for Northern India against Sind because he was not elected vice-captain, Dilawar Hussain having been given that honour. On that occasion two other players, Amir Elahi at present in England and Mubarak Ali refused to play in sympathy for him.

22. *Times of India* (23 June 1936).
23. Ibid.
24. Ibid.
25. Ibid.
26. Ibid.
27. The Board commended Vizzy for his gesture as evident from the following report published in the *Times of India*:

> The player seems to have recognized his offence and is willing to offer public apologies to the captain and manager and has solicited their indulgence. The captain was under the painful necessity to take the action he did and was bound by virtue of his position to preserve a dignified silence in the face of press antagonism. The captain will be delighted to let bygones be bygones and accede to the Board's request as he is extremely broadminded and does not bear any personal malice against the player concerned. The Maharajkumar of Vizianagram is willing to receive back the player now that the effect of the necessary disciplinary action has been felt.

28. *Times of India* (15 July 1936).
29. Ibid. (18 July 1936).
30. Ibid.
31. Ibid. (19 July 1936).
32. Ibid. (21 July 1936).
33. Ibid.
34. Ibid. Referring to the team Amarnath stated:

> You have seen the result of the Lancashire match and also the English press comments on Major Nayudu's captaincy. I can boldly say that every

member of the team would be glad to play under Nayudu. If we are to make any impression in the second Test we should field our best side and Nayudu should lead the side. Sitting here nobody has seen things as I have seen them and the Board of Control should adopt this suggestion immediately if they do not wish to be continually ridiculed. Our tactical errors in the field have been the target of English humour. Is it strict discipline or a joke that the captain of an international touring side should withdraw his own words twice? The whole episode should be judged by Duleepsinhji.

35. In fact he declared emphatically that he had no knowledge of the telegrams and demanded the production of the originals. He claimed that the telegram episode and the committee's attitude towards him had damaged his reputation. He emphasised that the committee had asked him no questions about the telegrams and had given him no opportunity to discuss the matter with them.

36. Amarnath captained the Indian team to Pakistan in 1952 and was the first Indian skipper to win a series abroad. For his bold attitude, Amarnath is remembered by all as the 'stormy petrel' of Indian cricket.

37. This function was held at the Wembley Conference Centre on 25 July 2002.

5. Nayudu Scorned

1. Vasant Raiji, *C.K. Nayudu: The Shahenshah of Indian Cricket* (Bombay: Marine Sports, 1989), p. xi.

2. Ibid., pp. 66–67.

3. For details see, *Wisden Cricketers Almanac* (London: John Wisden and Company, 1933). Nayudu's batsmanship had, in fact, become a symbol of colonial India's resistance against the British. It was an indication that Indians were capable of beating the British at their own game. His 153 against Arthur Gilligan's visiting MCC is part of Indian cricket folklore. This innings by Nayudu may be regarded as that 'moment of departure', when an indigenous brand of Indian nationalism 'took off' on the cricket field. The following description of this innings (Edward Docker, *History of Indian Cricket*, Macmillan: Delhi, 1976, pp. 2–3) would testify this point:

> Nayadu played circumspectly forward to two balls from Boyes then danced out to the next one and hit it back over the bowler's head and onto the pavilion roof. The crowd was stunned. Was that the first six ever hit by an Indian batsman against the MCC? How would the bowlers react to that? The next over Jai played quietly through the restless murmuring of the crowd and Boyes bowled again to Nayadu. Crack! Another six, this time to the right of the pavilion and not only did the ground burst into a tremendous sustained roar but even the umpires were seen to clap vigorously. At the other end now the same treatment was meted out to Astill—two balls met defensively, the next one dispatched

over the sightscreen and onto the maidan.... It was amazing how fast the news spread, considering the city was still without a wireless set. When Nayadu and Mahale returned to the wicket after lunch every tree was black with human spectators, every rooftop that commanded even a partial or distant view of the game.

4. Raiji, *C.K. Nayudu*, p. 21.
5. For details see, Boria Majumdar, 'A Star is Scorned', in *Wisden Asia Cricket* (Bombay: Spenta Publishing, November 2002).
6. Ibid.
7. Raiji, *C.K. Nayudu*, p. 59.
8. Ibid., p. 12.
9. For details of this controversy see, *Bombay Sentinel* (November–December 1937).
10. Ibid.
11. Raiji, *C.K. Nayudu*, p. 60.
12. Ibid.
13. Ibid.
14. Quoted in Majumdar, 'A Star is Scorned'.
15. Ibid.
16. Ibid.
17. Ibid.
18. Ibid.
19. Ibid.
20. Raiji, *C.K. Nayudu*, p. 60.
21. Ibid., p. xiv.
22. For details see, Majumdar, 'A Star is Scorned'.
23. Raiji, *C.K. Nayudu*, pp. 62–63.
24. For many such advertisements see, *Indian Cricket* (Bombay: Cricket Club of India, 1934–39).
25. Nayudu played his last match for the Maharashtra Governor's XI against the Maharashtra Chief Ministers XI at Nagpur in 1963, a week before his 68th birthday. In the first innings of the match he was unbeaten on 10 while in the second he was out for 1 caught by Abbas Ali Baig off the bowling of Ajit Wadekar. He bowled one over in this match conceding seven runs.

6. Tour de Farce

1. 'Rajputana Tour Discredits Indian Cricket', in the *Times of India* (30 June 1938).
2. J.C. Maitra, 'Unhappy Return of the Rajputana Team from England', in the *Bombay Chronicle* (17 July 1938).
3. Ibid.
4. Ibid.
5. 'Rajputana Cricket Tour to England', in the Anandji Dossa Collection (copy with the author).

6. *Bombay Chronicle* (17 July 1938).
7. *Times of India* (30 June 1938).
8. *Bombay Chronicle* (17 July 1938).
9. 'Rajputana Cricket Tour to England', in the Anandji Dossa Collection.
10. Ibid.
11. *Times of India* (30 June 1938).
12. Ibid.
13. *Bombay Chronicle* (17 July 1938).
14. 'Rajputana Cricket Tour to England', in the Anandji Dossa Collection. Bose was ably supported by Gopaldas who scored 76.
15. *Times of India* (6 July 1938). In a letter to the Editor of the *Times of India* dated 9 August 1938, the secretary of the Indian Gymkhana, David S. Erulkar, refuted the charge saying:

> With reference to the heading 'Rajputana Tour Discredits Indian Cricket' in the columns of your issue of 6 July last, I am desired, on behalf of the Indian Gymkhana Club to take exception to the following statement of your correspondent, 'The trouble originated... without the Gymkhana players having a chance to arrange themselves to act as hosts.' It is not known to the Committee where your correspondent got his information from about this decision of the Indian Gymkhana committee to which he refers, but I am to point out that there was no such decision whatsoever and the first time that this matter was placed before the committee, the payment for the luncheons and teas of the Rajputana team was sanctioned by the committee and actually paid for. Accordingly your correspondent's statement about the decision being conveyed in unfortunately worded terms is equally untrue as no such decision existed. Further, with regard to the two day match with the Rajputana team fixed for 20 and 21 July it was decided to bear the cost of the visiting teams' luncheons and teas for both days, but as the Rajputana team subsequently abandoned the tour, this match was not played.
>
> I might explain that as a rule the committee does not pay for luncheons and teas of visiting teams. Annually there are over sixty Home matches played by the Indian Gymkhana club teams, and if the committee were to sanction luncheon and tea expenses of all the visiting teams, it would be a very serious burden on the feeble finances of the club. The club incurred a debt of nearly 2000 pound in 1920 as the donations then collected fell short of the cost of purchasing and developing the property, and it is only in the beginning of this year that, thanks to certain generous donors, this long standing club debt has been wiped out.
>
> The revenue from subscriptions which is fixed at the low figure of 1 pound and 10 pence per year can hardly cover even a small portion of the running expenses of the club, and it would be hardly fair to fritter away sums donated to the club in entertaining visiting teams. These considerations have enforced a policy of strict economy and with that

view the committee has no other alternative but to expect the visiting teams to pay for their own luncheons and teas, and the fact that year after year so many matches have been arranged at the Gymkhana grounds without any difficulty would indicate that the visiting teams do not in any way resent such an arrangement. Further it would not be correct to assume that it is a recognized practice for the visiting teams to be entertained to luncheons and teas except in the case of return matches where hospitality is mutual.

The existence of our general rule may have been misinterpreted to cause the trouble to which your correspondent refers, but no decision of the committee to refuse luncheons and teas to the Rajputana team, as argued by your correspondent, was ever taken. It is greatly to be deplored that your correspondent should have indulged in such irresponsible and misleading statements seriously detrimental to the committee of the Indian Gymkhana Club, and mischievous in their implications.

16. 'Rajputana Cricket Tour to England', in the Anandji Dossa Collection.
17. Ibid.
18. Ibid.
19. *Bombay Chronicle* (17 July 1938).
20. *Times of India* (30 June 1938).
21. Ibid. (25 June 1938).
22. Ibid. (3 July 1938).
23. Ibid. (4 July 1938).
24. Ibid. (6 July 1938).
25. *Bombay Chronicle* (17 July 1938).
26. *Times of India* (6 July 1938).
27. *Bombay Chronicle* (17 July 1938).
28. Ibid.

7. The Pentangular Panned

1.   An Indian term for clubs. In pre-Partition India such clubs were community-based and cricket was organised along communitarian lines. Cricket in pre-Partition Bombay was dominated by these Gymkhanas, which were, in most cases, financially stable, due to the immense popularity of the Bombay Pentangular tournament organised by them.

2.   By the 1890s, the Parsees of Bombay had acquired considerable cricketing prowess and had no difficulty defeating the Europeans of the city. This led to a proposal that they should henceforth play a combined European team, comprising the best European talent in the Presidency. With encouragement from Lord Harris, Governor of Bombay between 1890–95, these matches were started in 1892. In the first year, however, the match was washed away because of rain and fire engines had to be brought to dry the ground, which led to the match becoming known as the Fire Engine match.

3. Initially the Pentangular was played in the monsoon months of July and August. It was shifted to the winter months in 1918. The tournament continued to be played in the last months of the year till 1944. In 1945, the tournament could not be held in December and was played in January. It was discontinued thereafter.

4. *Bombay Chronicle* (27 November 1935). For similar views see, *The Statesman* (2 December 1935); Berry Sarbadhikary, *Indian Cricket Uncovered* (Calcutta: Illustrated News, 1945).

5. Maitra continued to write against the communal Pentangular in his columns through the 1940s. When the tournament was eventually terminated, he expressed hope that its place would be successfully taken by a zonal Pentangular.

6. J.M. Ganguly, 'Quadrangular Cricket—A Plea for its Abolition', in *Indian Cricket* (Bombay: Cricket Club of India, April 1938), p. 188.

7. Berry Sarbadhikary, *Indian Cricket Uncovered*, pp. 60–61.

8. *Bombay Chronicle* (7 December 1940).

9. Ibid.

10. Ibid. (3 December 1940).

11. Ibid. (19 December 1940).

12. *Times of India* (10 December 1940). It is striking to note that the mounting of opposition to the Pentangular was accompanied by a simultaneous rise in the popularity of the tournament. Eyewitness accounts reveal that the stadium was packed to capacity in all matches of the Pentangular.

13. This is borne out by the description of the meeting published in the *Bombay Chronicle* (14 December 1940):

> After nearly three hours of storm and deafening clamour, the special General meeting of the P.J. Hindu Gymkhana, called to consider the issue of the Hindus participating in the Pentangular Cricket Tournament, decided by 280 votes to 243 that, the Hindu Gymkhana with whom lies the responsibility of putting in the field the Hindu XI for the Pentangular should not sponsor a side to play in the Pentangular, that starts at the Brabourne stadium today. There was intense excitement within and outside the Gymkhana. On the lawns of the Gymkhana assembled a large crowd largely composed of boys, who kept up shouting their slogan 'Hindus must play' and 'Stop drinking and gambling and then interfere with sport.' These youngsters were difficult to keep in hand as hooliganism and stone throwing were indulged in. The meeting itself was a most disorganised affair. Both camps, for and against, were determined to have their say at one and the same time. Shouting generally drowned every effort to speak out. A number of attempts were made to take the sense of the meeting but every time tactics to outwit a genuine vote frustrated the efforts. It was eventually decided to take count of opinions by making members leave the room one at a time after pronouncing their views on the issue.

14. *Times of India* (16 December 1940).

15. Ibid. (14 December 1940).
16. Ibid.
17. They also tried to put up a Hindu team ignoring the wishes of the Hindu Gymkhana. This effort was described at length in the *Bombay Chronicle* (20 December 1940):

    Today it is revealed that but for the want of the formal consent of the Bombay Pentangular Committee a Hindu team might have participated in this year's Pentangular. Following the meeting on December 13, a late effort was made to raise a Hindu side, a number of representatives of various Hindu clubs got together and decided to flout the authority of the Hindu Gymkhana and challenge the boycott decision. These clubs informally approached the Bombay Pentangular Committee. They were made to understand that a Hindu team if got together and was sufficiently representative, it would be accepted for participation. A new Hindu selection committee was formed, representatives of Bombay city, Maharastra, Baroda and Western Indian states being on the committee. This body, it is said, selected all the players previously chosen bar Vijay Merchant and L.P. Jai. Professor D.B. Deodhar was mentioned as Captain. But it was felt the Professor would stand down in favour of Major C.K. Nayadu, as this was the silver jubilee year of the major's cricketing career. A wire was sent to L. Amarnath to reach Bombay by last Tuesday morning. All these plans, however, fell through when the Bombay Pentangular committee met to consider the question. They withdrew their formal consent and decided by a majority that this new Hindu team should not be accepted.
18. *Times of India* (14 December 1940).
19. Ramachandra Guha, 'Cricket and Politics in Colonial India', *Past and Present*, 161 (November 1998), p. 183.
20. *Bombay Chronicle* (13 November 1941).
21. Ibid.
22. Guha, 'Cricket and Politics', pp. 186–87. Also see, Guha, *A Corner of a Foreign Field*.
23. Vasant Raiji and Mohandas Menon, *The Story of the Bombay Tournament: From Presidency to Pentangulars* (Mumbai: Ernest Publications, 2000), p. 93.
24. *Bombay Chronicle* (29 October 1946).
25. *Bombay Chronicle* (1 December 1941). Abdullah Brelvi referred to this fact in a public address. Curiously enough while he spoke of making a stand against the communal menace by banning the Pentangular, his own paper, the *Bombay Chronicle*, made no effort to boycott it. In fact, a report published in February 1948 draws attention to the fact that swimming baths in the city continued to be organised along communal lines:

    A sure consequence of the passing away of Mahatma Gandhi will be an untiring effort all over the country to end communalism in sport. The abolition of the Bombay Pentangular cricket, a communal tournament, which seemed to have an unfailing attraction in Western India, is a pointer to the future of all communal sport. There are, however, a number of private clubs and gymkhanas that close their doors to members of communities other than their own. At a moment when the cry against the communal Pentangular seemed to have borne fruit, a top ranking Congress leader declared open a Hindu swimming bath in the heart of Bombay! Membership of this club is, even at the moment, restricted to caste Hindus to the embarrassment and discomfiture of the average sportsman in the city.

If government were sincere about abolishing the last traces of communalism in sport, if they mean to respect the memory of India's grand old prophet, they could pay him no better tribute than abolishing sports bodies that tend to favour a particular community to the exclusion of brother sportsmen around. For here in sport, as is no other visible sphere of existence, is a possible panacea to much of the discord evident in other spheres of life. If government made it obligatory on the part of every sports body to refrain from discrimination in respect of membership, there is every chance of our having just one single community—a community of sportsmen. *Sport and Pastime* (14 February 1948).

26. *Bombay Chronicle* (2 December 1944).
27. Ibid. (16 December 1940).
28. Ibid. (16 December 1940).
29. Sarbadhikary, *Indian Cricket Uncovered*, pp. 71–72. It was natural for the United Provinces Cricket Association to oppose the commercially viable Pentangular given its miserable financial state. On 16 December 1940 a select delegation of the United Provinces Cricket Association had met the Governor of the United Provinces drawing his attention to the impoverished financial state plaguing the association. The deputation requested the Governor to raise the non-recurring grant of Rs. 500 to Rs. 1000, making it a recurring grant in the process. The deputationists, the *Bombay Chronicle* states, pointed out that there was a woeful lack of sustained general interest in the game in the province and hoped that with the reorganisation of the association things will improve. A couple of days later Vizzy, the President of the Association referred to the financial crisis facing the association, which had made the holding of trial matches difficult. It was not unnatural that he voiced his criticism against the Pentangular the very next day, 19 December 1940. *Bombay Chronicle* (16, 18 and 19 December 1940).
30. *Times Of India* (23 November 1943).
31. Proceedings of the Extra-Ordinary General Meeting of the Board held on 22 January 1942 with Dr. Subbaraon as the chair. Mr. Mansur Alam, representative of the United Provinces Cricket Association, tabled the resolution. The resolution was originally in two parts, but the second, calling for the imposition of a penalty upon players who participated in communal

tournaments, was eventually dropped. Muni Lal (ed.), *The Crickinia: 1942–43* (Lahore, published by the author, 1943), pp. 65–66.

32. Mr. Contractor declared that the resolution was *ultra vires* as there was no clause in Rule 2 of the Board's constitution that empowered it to interfere in the internal affairs of a provincial association.

33. Ranga Rao, representing the Madras Cricket Association moved a second amendment. Like the first, it wanted the question of the continuance or discontinuance of the Pentangular to be examined by a sub-committee appointed by the Board, in which the Bombay and United Provinces Cricket Associations were adequately represented.

34. Proceedings of the Extra-Ordinary General Meeting of the Board held on 22 January 1942, *The Crickinia: 1942–43*, pp. 67–68.

35. Ibid.

36. Dr. Subbaraon went on to say that it was a matter of pleasure to note that the Princes had become national-minded and were trying to do away with communalism in every branch of life. This, he thought, would help in laying the foundation of a free India.

37. This was a victory for the Bombay Cricket Association. The Board was forced to persuade Mr. Mansur Alam and Mr. Pankaj Gupta to withdraw their amendments in the wake of tremendous opposition from the members of the Bombay Cricket Association.

38. Proceedings of the Communal Cricket Sub-Committee, *The Crickinia: 1942–43*, pp. 76–78.

39. Minutes of dissent against the resolutions passed by the Communal Cricket Sub-Committee, *The Crickinia: 1942–43*, pp. 81–83.

40. Ibid., pp. 83–84.

41. *Times Of India* (23 November 1942). The same report goes on to state that even after a Bombay sportsman had offered to make up for the losses suffered by the Bombay Cricket Association, it refused to participate in the national championships.

42. *Times Of India* (23 November 1942). Merchant's stand assumes great significance in view of his statements issued in favour of the Pentangular a couple of years later. He was forthright in declaring that of all the cricket tournaments held in Bombay, the Pentangular was the only source of income to the cricket organisation in the city. Responding to the criticism that it fostered communal ill feeling, he referred to his experiences after the 1936 tournament. He went on to state 'It may come as a very great surprise to you when I tell you that during the ten days the Quadrangular was played, not a single incident took place in the whole of Bombay, and immediately after the tournament was over the communal riot sub-sided.' It is no surprise, therefore, that Merchant was fully supportive of the Bombay Cricket Association in its tussle against the Board.

43. Ibid. (16 November 1942).

44. Berry Sarbadhikary, 'Thoughts on Zonal Cricket', in *Sport and Pastime* (11 December 1948).

8. The Pretender and the Prima Donna

1. 'Cricket Changes', in the *Times of India* (7 August 1951).
2. *Times of India* (15 April 1949).
3. Ibid.
4. Ibid. (7 May 1949).
5. Ibid. (19 April 1949).
6. Ibid.
7. Ibid. (9 May 1949).
8. Ibid. (10 May 1949).
9. Ibid.
10. Ibid. (6 May 1949).
11. Ibid.
12. 'Mud Slinging in Indian Cricket', in the *Sunday News of India* (12 June 1949).
13. *Times of India* (6 June 1949).
14. *National Standard* (30 June 1949). The 18th instalment of the series went thus:

> *Mr. De Mello's charge number 20*
> Your statement at a lunch in Bombay on 9th February charging the Board with 'Power Politics' was reported by the UPI.
>
> *Captain Amarnath's reply*
> It is incorrect that I made any reference to 'power politics' at a lunch in Bombay on 9 February, which I gave in honour of the West Indies cricketers. I did, however, give an interview to the United Press of India on 11 February in Bombay after the last Test was over. Almost the entire interview dealt with the technical aspects of Test cricket and an appreciation of the West Indies cricketers. In answer to a question on the organisation of our cricket with a view to India taking her rightful place in international cricket I used the expression 'Power Politics' in a very general way.

The 17th was even more interesting:

> *Mr. De Mello's charge number 19*
> Your not sitting with your team for lunch during the fifth Test match at Bombay.
>
> *Captain Amarnath's reply*
> It is not true that I did not sit with my team for lunch in the whole of the fifth Test at Bombay. As far as I remember I missed the lunch only once or twice.
>
> It is surprising that Mr. De Mello has made my not sitting with the team once or twice during the fifth Test match the subject of a charge against an Indian captain who led the country in Australia for about five

months on a tour, which, if nothing else, was considered a great social success and then again in India against the West Indies. Throughout the series I have made it a point to attend most of the lunches with my team.

If Mr. De Mello means that my not sitting with my team so very occasionally was discourteous either to my team or my guests, it is wholly untrue. In fact, I always asked Mr. John Goddard but he came to lunch very occasionally throughout the Test series. I do not know what you think of it, but I think it is trivial, except for those who must frame a charge sheet against someone at all costs.

15. *Sunday Standard* (3 July 1949).
16. *National Standard* (9 July 1949).
17. *Sunday News of India* (24 July 1949).
18. *National Standard* (25 July 1949).
19. *Times of India* (30 July 1949).
20. *Sunday News of India* (31 July 1949).
21. For details see, Boria Majumdar, 'Mr. De Mello's Axe', in *Wisden Asia Cricket* (January 2003).
22. *Times of India* (5 April 1950).
23. Ibid.
24. Ibid. (12 August 1951).
25. Ibid.
26. Ibid.
27. Ibid. (8 August 1951).
28. For details see, Boria Majumdar, 'A Sticky End', in *Wisden Asia Cricket* (February 2003).
29. Ibid.
30. *Times of India* (12 October 1952).
31. Ibid.
32. Ibid.
33. Ibid.
34. Ibid.
35. Ibid.
36. Majumdar, 'A Sticky End'.
37. *Times of India* (6 October 1952).
38. Ibid. (13 October 1952).
39. Quoted in Majumdar, 'A Sticky End'.

9. Mankad's Folly

1. A report published in the *Times of India* on 13 January 1952 declared, 'All rounder Vinoo Mankad, the first Indian cricketer to turn professional has notified the Board of Control for Cricket in India that he will not be available for inclusion in the Indian team to tour England this summer.'

2. For details see, Boria Majumdar, 'The Mankad Imbroglio', in *Wisden Asia Cricket* (March 2003).

3. 'Vijay Hazare to Captain: Board's Vote Unanimous', in the *Times of India* (18 February 2003).

4. In fact, in a report filed from Colombo the correspondent of the *Times of India* declared on 16 February 1952:

> India's Test all rounder Vinoo Mankad stated today that his decision to retire from Test cricket at the end of his career was 'absolutely final.' He added that, he would, however, continue as a professional in first class cricket. Asked why he has taken such a decision at a time when he was at the peak of his form, Mankad declared, 'A sportsman must retire when he is at his best and give young men a chance.' Mankad, who is here on the invitation of the Ceylon Cricket Board to play for the Commonwealth side against the MCC said he would be only too glad to play for India in Tests in England next summer if selected by India and subject to release by the Haslingden Club, for who he plays in the Lancashire league. Mankad said that he would be willing to take up a position as a professional cricket coach in Ceylon if an approach was made to him by the Ceylon Cricket Board and the terms were agreeable. Informed of this, the Cricket Board Secretary, Mr. K.M. Ismail said, 'Ceylon indeed needs a first class coach to improve her standard of cricket. I shall certainly discuss the matter with Mankad and report to my committee.'

5. 'Ceylon may give Vinoo Coaching Job', in the *Times of India* (20 February 1952).

6. *Times of India* (18 February 2003).

7. 'Board President declares there is no hanky panky in the controlling body', in the *Times of India* (10 March 1952).

8. Ibid. (20 April 1952).

9. Ibid. (3 June 1952).

10. Ibid.

11. Ibid. (5 June 1952).

12. Ibid.

13. Ibid. (2 June 1952).

14. Ibid.

15. The correspondent of the *Times of India* on 3 June 1952, emphasised the apprehensions of the Haslingden Club saying:

> As I write no word has come as yet of Haslingden's reaction to the request for Vinoo's release for the Tests. Personally, I doubt whether he will be allowed to assist India. In any case, if sufficient pressure is brought to bear on the club, his services will be made available, but only for the Leeds match. All in all, it is a regrettable affair, and the manner in which the Board of Control for Cricket in India has handled it confirms my view that our parent body as a whole does not possess as much sense

as the nearest competent junior in the fine old institution next door, Anjuman-I-Islam High School.

16. Ibid. (12 June 1952).
17. Ibid. (11 June 1952).
18. Ibid.
19. Ibid.
20. Ibid.
21. Ibid. (12 June 1952).
22. Ibid. (27 June 1952).
23. Ibid.
24. Ibid.
25. Ibid. (10 December 1952).
26. Ibid. (12 June 1952).
27. Ibid. (8 November 1952).
28. Ibid.
29. Ibid.
30. Ibid. (18 December 1952).
31. Ibid. (24 December 1952).
32. Ibid.
33. Ibid. (21 December 1952).
34. Ibid. (6 November 1952).

10. Men in Black and White

1. Quoted in C. Sujit Chandra Kumar, Mark Mccleland and V.K. Shashikumar, 'Mere Puppets', in The Week (25 October 1998).
2. As Venkatraghvan mentioned:

   More than players, it is the TV that puts the pressure on the umpires. They live with the nagging feeling after every little decision of theirs that the camera may have called their bluff. Because, after play comes replay. Not one but a battalion from various angles.

   For details see, the Week (25 October 1998).
3. National Grid, replaced later by the Emirates Airline, sponsored the ICC panel of umpires.
4. Sir Donald Bradman rated Frank Chester as the finest umpire under whose supervision he had played. Chester did not have the services of an arm because of a war injury. But as Bradman said, 'He gave a decision after much deliberation and in most cases these were spot on. Anyone who had the pleasure of playing with Chester in charge knew that he would be fair and in most cases right.'
5. Bird became an umpire in 1970 and three years later officiated at his first Test match. At the beginning of his 66th and final test in 1996, the two teams—India and England—formed a 'guard of honour' as he came out and he received a standing ovation from the crowd.

6. One of the most respected and liked umpires in international cricket. He was appointed to the first-class list in 1981. After umpiring in the 1983 World Cup, he was appointed to his first Test in 1985. He stood in the 1987 and 1992 World Cups, and has the distinction of officiating at the finals of the 1996, 1999 and 2003 World Cups.

7. Nicknamed 'Slow Death Bucknor', he has umpired in more Test matches than anyone else. Has the rare distinction of standing in four World Cup finals, 1992, 1996, 1999 and 2003.

8. Venkatraghavan, the former Indian cricket captain, is the only man in the game's history to have played over 50 Tests and to have umpired more than 50 Tests.

9. Hair, the most outspoken among modern umpires, became famous when he no-balled Muralitharan seven times for throwing during the Melbourne Test in 1995 and again when he said in his autobiography that he could have no-balled him many more times.

10. Commenting on his 'hop', Shepherd states:

> A lot of people are quite familiar with one of my superstitions, the little hop I give when the score passes certain milestones. It harks back to when I was a kid playing village cricket down in Devon and we had an unlucky number—111. We call it The Nelson, which you would also get with other multiples like 222 and 333. We found that the only way to counteract something bad happening on a Nelson number was to get your feet off the ground. You could just lift your feet off the pavilion floor if you weren't in the middle, but if I was on the field of play I would just jump or hop. I would usually jump, but maybe hop depending on what time of day it is, how long I've been out there or how hot the weather is. When I took to umpiring, I thought I couldn't keep doing that, but a few mates urged me to carry on and not many people noticed it at the time. Then I did it in my second Test match at Edgbaston and someone wrote into dear old Brian Johnston on Test Match Special and he let the cat out of the bag. I've been stuck with it ever since! Sometimes I miss it when I'm too wrapped up with what's happening on the field. I can't think of any other umpires with superstitions like that. Perhaps there's only one idiot!

See news.bbc.co.uk/sport/hi/english/static/in_depth/cricket/2001/ashes/umpire_guide/quirks.stm.

11. One of India's best known umpires, he officiated in Test matches during 1978–85 and in one-day internationals during 1981–85.

12. Even in recent times, as reported by the *Week*:

> There are so many qualified and experienced umpires in the south and west zones that to get an international match is like hitting the jackpot. 'The selection of umpires for the international matches is very bad,' said ex-Indian player Bharat Reddy. Often raw hands get the nod while

experienced umpires sit at home. Many umpires in different parts of the country are disgruntled.

For details see, Kumar, Mccleland and Shashikumar, 'Mere Puppets'.

13. For details of this match see, P.B. Jog, *How's that? 'Board of Control' Out* (Bombay, published by the author, 1964), p. 12.
14. Ibid., pp. 17–18.
15. *Times of India* (26 January 1958).
16. Jog, *How's that?*, pp. 18–20.
17. Ibid., p. 6.
18. Ibid., pp. 20–21.
19. Ibid., pp. 25–28.
20. Ibid., pp. 23–24.
21. Ibid., pp. 29–30.
22. Ibid., p. 30.
23. *Times of India* (15 January 1964).
24. Jog, *How's that?*, pp. 37–38.

11. Match Fixing

1. Rudrangshu Mukherjee, in *The Telegraph* (4 November 2000).
2. Quoted in Boria Majumdar, 'Indian Cricket—Myths and Reality', in www.outlookindia.com (7 March 2001).
3. Ibid.
4. One of the central characters of cricket's romantic lore is W.G. Grace, hailed as the father of cricket. A man for whom the laws of cricket were moulded, whose personality generated the largest number of cricketing anecdotes and is idealised as the epitome of a virtuous generation. While these myths around Grace are the stuff of a cricket fan's nostalgia, the reality could leave him/her shell-shocked. W.G. was the best-known gentleman cricketer. Definitionally, the latter phrase refers to an amateur athlete comfortable enough not to accept money to play. W.G., however, received £3,000 as his fee during the 1893 tour to Australia, not an exceptional feat in his long 44-year career. In an age where a number of outstanding amateurs were forced to shorten their cricketing careers in favour of more lucrative pursuits, any attempt by Grace's followers to exonerate their hero from the charge of deceit is unacceptable. This provokes Simon Rae to write in Grace's latest biography, *W.G. Grace—A Life*:

> Though often depicted as an overgrown schoolboy, W.G. was extremely shrewd and ruthlessly exploited the power his immense popularity gave him. A notorious 'shamateur' he amassed great wealth through cricket while remaining the standard bearer for the gentleman against the players for forty years.

5. G. Rajaraman, 'Match Fixing—A Dead Enemy', in Boria Majumdar and J.A. Mangan (eds.), *Cricketing Cultures in Conflict—World Cup 2003* (Routledge,

London, 2004). Former Indian captain Lala Amarnath narrated this incident to Rajaraman's father N. Ganesan, who retired after being a sports journalist, first-class cricket umpire and cricket administrator. The informal interview took place in Rajaraman's apartment in Delhi before Amarnath passed away at the age of 88 on 5 August 2000.

6. Ibid.
7. One of the oldest tournaments in the country, the Kanga league has unearthed many talented cricketers. Playing in the Kanga league is considered a cricketer's basic education in Bombay cricket circles.
8. A.C. Perreira, 'The Khot Incident: Was he Guilty', in the *Sunday News of India* (6 October 1948).
9. For details see, Majumdar, 'Indian Cricket—Myths and Reality'.

12. All the Skipper's Men

1. For details see, *The Telegraph* (7 August 1989).
2. Ibid.
3. Quoted in the *Asian Recorder* (12–18 November 1989), pp. 20869– 70.
4. Ibid.
5. Ibid.
6. Ibid.
7. Lokendra Pratap Sahi, 'Telling Blow to Player Power', in *The Telegraph* (7 August 1989).
8. *The Telegraph* (15 September 1989).
9. *Asian Recorder* (12–18 November 1989), pp. 20869–70.
10. *The Telegraph* (15 September 1989).
11. Ibid.

Epilogue

1. Sorabjee, *A Chronicle of Cricket Among Parsees and The Struggle: Polo verses Cricket*, p. 26.
2. *Indian Cricket*, February 1936, p. 54.
3. *Free Press Journal* (18 October 1950). In the same report, the author mentions that Bombay had served host to Gilligan's team in 1926–27, Jardine's team in 1933–34 and the Australian side brought out by the Maharaja of Patiala in 1935–36, but for all these matches the costs to Bombay as a whole were nowhere near the figure that was now being claimed by the BCCI for the one Test allotted to Bombay.
4. Ibid. (13 October 1950).
5. *Times of India* (22 July 1951).
6. Ibid. (21 July 1951). This proposal was mooted by the President of the BCCI, A.S. De Mello, who was of the view that whenever a foreign team

visited India, the Ranji Trophy matches were delayed, the completion of the tournament eventually becoming a matter of grave concern. It became a matter of inconvenience for the players and posed enormous difficulties to the host centre.

7. *Free Press Journal* (14 May 1950).
8. *Times of India* (28 April 1952). Though the Club of Maharashtra and the PYC Hindu Gymkhana came forward to help the schools after the Government's decision was announced, their efforts could hardly compensate the loss. Moreover, the Club of Maharashtra charged a fee of Rs. 25 for its coaching camp that was beyond the reach of many.
9. *Sport and Pastime* (7 August 1948).

Index